# A SPEAKER'S TREASURY

# A SPEAKER'S TREASURY

**FOR EDUCATORS, CONVOCATION SPEAKERS, BACCALAUREATE SPEAKERS, COMMENCEMENT SPEAKERS, PTA OFFICERS, SCHOOL BOARD MEMBERS, AND OTHERS**

Herbert V. Prochnow

BAKER BOOK HOUSE
GRAND RAPIDS, MICHIGAN

ISBN: 0-8010-6937-8

© 1973 by Baker Book House Company

Printed in the United States of America

# Preface

With over one thousand items, this book is meant to be helpful to many groups, and an especially valuable reference for students and teachers. Among the items are hundreds of witticisms and humorous stories which will not only add zest to speeches, writing, and conversation, but are also fun to read just for themselves.

There are unusual excerpts from baccalaureate, commencement, and other addresses which will be useful in the preparation of remarks for similar occasions. In addition, there are many inspiring quotations from literature which may effectively stress a point or clothe an illustration in the most colorful language.

The book has dozens of illustrations from interesting lives. These stories portray vividly many of the experiences of human life. Finally, there are included a large number of the best thoughts of the great minds of the world. Here then is a book which deals with a wide range of subjects that should make it a source of reference on many occasions.

All those who must from time to time make brief remarks, deliver a speech, or preside at meetings should find the use of these source materials rewarding.

The book has grown not only out of the practical experience of high school and university teaching, but also out of the experience of addressing high school and university commencements, business and banking meetings, service clubs, and professional societies.

Although many stories and illustrations may be adapted for different situations, a comprehensive index in the back of the book will be of assistance in the selection of pertinent items.

If the book should prove interesting to the general reader who appreciates a humorous quip or story, or an inspiring illustration, and more specifically if it proves helpful to those who speak or preside at meetings, it will have served the purpose for which it was planned.

*Herbert V. Prochnow*

# Contents

# Part One

---

## QUIPS AND WITTICISMS

# Quips and Witticisms

□ Tomorrow is the day that comes before we know how to handle today's problems. *Herbert V. Prochnow*

□ When you are busy rowing the boat, you don't have much time to rock it.

□ The danger in an affluent society is that people can be better off without being better.

□ It's hard to take advice from persons you know need it worse than you do. *Herbert V. Prochnow*

□ If you get some hard bumps, it at least shows you are out of the rut.

□ A great many people would not only like to eat their cake and have it too, but also get the other fellow's cake.

□ The way to get the last word in an argument is to say, "I agree."

□ No two of us are alike and we are both glad of it. *Herbert V. Prochnow*

11

□ Opportunity doesn't knock these days; it rings the phone and an interviewer asks a silly question.

□ Few of us take advantage of our opportunities to keep quiet.
*Herbert V. Prochnow*

□ In the beginning God brought order out of chaos and since then man has been trying to reverse the situation.

□ Some college freshmen talked for twelve hours in a telephone marathon. We wish we could do something great like that.

□ Few persons ever grow up. They merely change their playthings.

□ We never could understand why rock and roll musicians get paid more than riveters.

□ As the sixth grade youngster said, "the plural of child is twins."

□ We can amplify the human voice many times, but we seem unable to do anything for the still small voice of conscience.
*Herbert V. Prochnow*

□ You will be successful if you plan carefully and don't have quite enough time to do a job.

□ Most people who join committees probably do so on the theory that it's easier to endorse an idea than to understand it.

□ Only an average person is always at his best.

□ Twenty minutes should be long enough for a speaker to tell what he knows, but sometimes he gets more interesting after that.

□ The fellow without a college education at least doesn't have to look forward to possible disaster every Saturday afternoon in the football season.

□ A psychologist says a healthy mind doubts everything which hasn't been proved, but we doubt this.

□ It's about time the meek inherited the earth when you consider the mess the unmeek have made of it.

□ No football team is so good that it satisfies the alumni or the Monday morning quarterbacks.

□ If you want to flatter almost anyone, just look serious and ask him what he thinks of the world situation.

□ Most speeches have a happy ending—everyone is glad when they are over.

□ We can't understand why some persons won't admit their faults. We would if we had any.                    *Herbert V. Prochnow*

□ Nature didn't make us perfect, so she did the next best thing— she made us blind to our faults.          *Herbert V. Prochnow*

□ Some co-eds said they intend to marry "men of brains, character, adequate incomes, and a nice sense of humor." It sounds like bigamy.

◻ America is a great rich country where everyone wants something from the government besides government.

◻ If we could see ourselves as others see us, we wouldn't believe it.

◻ One thing all nations have in common is the ability to see each other's faults.

◻ The optimist may be wrong but he has a lot more fun than the pessimist.                                            *Herbert V. Prochnow*

◻ When all of us are in agreement, we are almost always wrong.

◻ With the guarantee of free speech we sometimes wish we had a way to guarantee its quality.

◻ You really have insomnia if you can't sleep when it's time to get up.

◻ There are two kinds of people, the good and the bad, and the good ones are like you and me.

◻ In the good old days only one man in the world thought he was Napoleon.

◻ A luxury is something you don't really need and can't do without.

◻ An egotist is a person who is fascinated with himself.

☐ If you would like to live a quiet, peaceful, uneventful life, you are living at the wrong time.

☐ Everyone makes mistakes but some persons give them assistance.

☐ Faster and more frequent mail service seems desirable until you see what you are getting.

☐ It's sort of depressing to think that most of us are just like the rest of the people. *Herbert V. Prochnow*

☐ The college graduate thinks he is going to run the world some day and the interesting fact is that he is.

☐ What we dislike is a speaker who doesn't know much but knows it fluently.

☐ An old-timer is a person who can remember when the visual equipment for teaching child psychology was a shingle.

☐ A professor is one who talks in someone else's sleep.
*Wystan Hugh Auden*

☐ What's all our knowledge worth? We don't even know what the weather will be tomorrow. *Berthold Auerbach*

☐ She's generous to a fault—if it's her own. *Arthur Baer*

☐ Repartee is what you wish you'd said. *Heywood Broun*

□ He had insomnia so bad that he couldn't sleep when he was working. *Arthur Baer*

□ If *Hamlet* had been written in these days it would probably have been called *The Strange Affair at Elsinore*.
*James Matthew Barrie*

□ We are all of us failures—at least, the best of us are.
*James Matthew Barrie*

□ Accustomed as I am to public speaking, I know the futility of it. *Franklin Pierce Adams*

□ If a man keeps his trap shut, the world will beat a path to his door. *Franklin Pierce Adams*

□ It is impossible to underrate human intelligence—beginning with one's own. *Henry Adams*

□ Authors have established it as a kind of rule that a man ought to be dull sometimes. *Joseph Addison*

□ Early to bed and early to rise, and you'll meet very few of our best people. *George Ade*

□ My father sent me to an engineering school to prepare me for a literary career. *George Ade*

□ After being turned down by numerous publishers, he decided to write for posterity. *George Ade*

□ It is easier to fight for one's principles than to live up to them.
*Alfred Adler*

□ The English instinctively admire any man who has no talent and is modest about it.
*James Agate*

□ Her hat is a creation that will never go out of style; it will just look ridiculous year after year.
*Fred Allen*

□ If a circus is half as good as it smells, it's a great show.
*Fred Allen*

□ It is amazing how nice people are to you when they know you are going away.
*Michael Arlen*

□ I was a modest, good-humored boy; it is Oxford that has made me insufferable.
*Max Beerbohm*

□ Drawing on my fine command of language, I said nothing.
*Robert Benchley*

□ It took me fifteen years to discover I had no talent for writing.
*Robert Benchley*

□ It was one of those plays in which all the actors unfortunately enunciated very clearly.
*Robert Benchley*

□ Merely having an open mind is nothing; the object of opening the mind, as of opening the mouth, is to shut it again on something solid.
*Gilbert Keith Chesterton*

◻ Good taste is better than bad taste, but bad taste is better than no taste at all.          *Arnold Bennett*

◻ It is well, when one is judging a friend, to remember that he is judging you with the same godlike and superior impartiality.          *Arnold Bennett*

◻ Bore: a person who talks when you wish him to listen.          *Ambrose Bierce*

◻ The fact that boys are allowed to exist at all is evidence of a remarkable Christian forbearance among men.          *Ambrose Bierce*

◻ A dog is the only thing on this earth that loves you more than he loves himself.          *John Billings*

◻ Silence is one of the hardest arguments to refute.          *Joseph Billings*

◻ Behind every argument is someone's ignorance.          *Louis Dembitz Brandeis*

◻ Shakespeare was a dramatist of note who lived by writing things to quote.          *Henry Cuyler Bunner*

◻ For those who do not think, it is best at least to rearrange their prejudices once in a while.          *Luther Burbank*

◻ The brain is a wonderful organ; it starts working the moment you get up in the morning, and does not stop until you get into the office.          *Robert Frost*

□ Wise men learn more from fools than fools from wise men.

*Marcus Porcius Cato*

□ He's all buttoned up in an impenetrable little coat of complacency.

*Ilka Chase*

□ The less one has to do, the less time one finds to do it in.

*Lord Chesterfield*

□ An expert is one who knows more and more about less and less.

*Nicholas Murray Butler*

□ By working faithfully eight hours a day, you may eventually get to be a boss and work twelve hours a day.

*Robert Frost*

□ Half the world is composed of people who have something to say and can't, and the other half who have nothing to say and keep on saying it.

*Robert Frost*

□ The reason why worry kills more people than work is that more people worry than work.

*Robert Frost*

□ The world is full of willing people; some willing to work, the rest willing to let them.

*Robert Frost*

□ You've no idea what a poor opinion I have of myself, and how little I deserve it.

*William Schwenck Gilbert*

□ After a fellow gets famous it doesn't take long for someone to bob up that used to sit by him at school.

*Frank McKinney Hubbard*

◻ In those days he was wiser than he is now; he used frequently to take my advice.　*Winston Churchill*

◻ Men occasionally stumble over the truth, but most of them pick themselves up and hurry off as if nothing had happened.　*Winston Churchill*

◻ If you don't say anything, you won't be called on to repeat it.　*Calvin Coolidge*

◻ A fool must now and then be right by chance.　*William Cowper*

◻ He was distinguished for ignorance; for he had only one idea and that was wrong.　*Benjamin Disraeli*

◻ My idea of an agreeable person is a person who agrees with me.　*Benjamin Disraeli*

◻ All generalizations are dangerous, even this one.　*Alexandre Dumas*

◻ Man is ready to die for an idea, provided that idea is not quite clear to him.　*Paul Eldridge*

◻ If fifty million people say a foolish thing, it is still a foolish thing.　*Anatole France*

◻ Everything bows to success, even grammar.　*Victor Hugo*

◻ The person who thinks he has no faults has at least one.

□ He that falls in love with himself will have no rivals.
*Benjamin Franklin*

□ The college graduate is presented with a sheepskin to cover his intellectual nakedness.     *Robert Maynard Hutchins*

□ If a little knowledge is dangerous, where is the man who has so much as to be out of danger?     Thomas Henry Huxley

□ There are two kinds of fools: one says, "This is old, therefore it is good"; the other says, "This is new, therefore it is better."
*William Ralph Inge*

□ When you have to make a choice and don't make it, that is in itself a choice.     *William James*

□ Everything comes to him who waits except a loaned book.
*Frank McKinney Hubbard*

□ Who recalls when folks got along without something if it cost too much?     *Frank McKinney Hubbard*

□ It is impossible to enjoy idling thoroughly unless one has plenty of work to do.     *Jerome K. Jerome*

□ Adversity is the state in which a man most easily becomes acquainted with himself, being especially free from admirers then.
*Samuel Johnson*

□ It's impossible to push yourself ahead by patting yourself on the back.     *Herbert V. Prochnow*

◻ Education is what remains when we have forgotten all that we have been taught. *George S. Halifax*

◻ If the Romans had been obliged to learn Latin, they would never have found time to conquer the world. *Heinrich Heine*

◻ Zoo: a place devised for animals to study the habits of human beings. *Oliver Herford*

◻ Your ignorance cramps my conversation. *Anthony Hope*

◻ If you think before you speak, the other fellow gets in his joke first. *Edgar Watson Howe*

◻ Most people put off till tomorrow that which they should have done yesterday. *Edgar Watson Howe*

◻ No man needs a vacation so much as the person who has just had one. *Elbert Hubbard*

◻ You can lead a boy to college but you cannot make him think. *Elbert Hubbard*

◻ He was dull in a new way, and that made many think him great. *Samuel Johnson*

◻ The time he can spare from the adornment of his person he devotes to the neglect of his duties. *Benjamin Jowett*

◻ Lawyers are men who hire out their words and anger. *Martial*

□ Your manuscript is both good and original; but the part that is good is not original, and the part that is original is not good.

*Samuel Johnson*

□ Life can only be understood backwards, but it must be lived forwards.                               *Sören Aabye Kierkegaard*

□ Gardens are not made by singing, "Oh, how beautiful," and sitting in the shade.                               *Rudyard Kipling*

□ The best way to get on in the world is to make people believe it's to their advantage to help you.             *Jean de La Bruyere*

□ A bore is a man who spends so much time talking about himself that you can't talk about yourself.           *Melville D. Landon*

□ He missed an invaluable opportunity to hold his tongue.

*Andrew Lang*

□ They gave each other a smile with a future in it.

*Ring Lardner*

□ In the misfortune of our best friends we find something which is not displeasing to us.       *Francois de La Rochefoucauld*

□ I was not accustomed to flattery; I was like the Hoosier who loved gingerbread better than any man and got less of it.

*Abraham Lincoln*

□ He who devotes sixteen hours a day to hard study may become as wise at sixty as he thought himself at twenty.

*Mary Wilson Little*

□ We confess little faults in order to suggest that we have no big ones. *Francois de La Rochefoucauld*

□ When I wish I was rich, then I know I am ill. *David Herbert Lawrence*

□ It's called political economy because it has nothing to do with either politics or economy. *Stephen Leacock*

□ I am a great believer in luck, and I find the harder I work the more I have of it. *Stephen Leacock*

□ I've given up reading books; I find it takes my mind off myself. *Oscar Levant*

□ For people who like that kind of a book, that is the kind of a book they will like. *Abraham Lincoln*

□ No man has a good enough memory to make a successful liar. *Abraham Lincoln*

□ There is no pleasure in having nothing to do; the fun is in having lots to do and not doing it. *Mary Wilson Little*

□ Universities are full of knowledge; the freshmen bring a little in and the seniors take none away, and knowledge accumulates. *Abbot Lawrence Lowell*

□ When he who hears doesn't know what he who speaks means, and when he who speaks doesn't know what he himself means— that is philosophy. *Voltaire*

24

□ Blessed are they who have nothing to say, and who cannot be persuaded to say it.                                 *James Russell Lowell*

□ It was a book to kill time for those who like it better dead.
                                                                                *Rose Macaulay*

□ Fishing is a delusion entirely surrounded by liars in old clothes.
                                                                                *Don Marquis*

□ If you make people think they're thinking, they'll love you; but if you really make them think, they'll hate you.     *Don Marquis*

□ An idea isn't responsible for the people who believe in it.
                                                                                *Don Marquis*

□ "Be yourself!" is about the worst advice you can give to some people.                                               *Tom Masson*

□ A senior always feels like the university is going to the kids.
                                                                                *Tom Masson*

□ A highbrow is a person educated beyond his intelligence.
                                                                                *Brander Matthews*

□ Conscience: the inner voice which warns us that someone may be looking.                                            *H. L. Mencken*

□ Argument is the worst sort of conversation.     *Jonathan Swift*

□ Everybody is ignorant, only on different subjects.     *Will Rogers*

◻ Some people's genius lies in giving infinite pains.

*Addison Mizner*

◻ A good listener is not only popular everywhere, but after a while he knows something. *Wilson Mizner*

◻ When you take stuff from one writer, it's plagiarism; but when you take it from many writers, it's research. *Wilson Mizner*

◻ For more than forty years I have been speaking prose without knowing it. *Moliere*

◻ There is only one rule for being a good talker: learn to listen.

*Christopher Morley*

◻ An Englishman thinks seated; a Frenchman, standing; an American, pacing; an Irishman, afterward. *Austin O'Malley*

◻ A hole is nothing at all, but you can break your neck in it.

*Austin O'Malley*

◻ I like criticism, but it must be my way. *Mark Twain*

◻ A conservative is a man with two perfectly good legs who has never learned to walk. *Franklin Delano Roosevelt*

◻ Common sense is not so common. *Voltaire*

◻ A guilty conscience is the mother of invention. *Carolyn Wells*

□ Be not simply good; be good for something.

*Henry David Thoreau*

□ All you need in this life is ignorance and confidence, and then success is sure. *Mark Twain*

□ Always do right; this will gratify some people and astonish the rest. *Mark Twain*

□ If you tell the truth, you don't have to remember anything.

*Mark Twain*

□ It usually takes me more than three weeks to prepare a good impromptu speech. *Mark Twain*

□ The Difficult is that which can be done immediately; the Impossible that which takes a little longer. *George Santayana*

□ It is difficult to keep quiet if you have nothing to do.

*Arthur Schopenhauer*

□ If all economists were laid end to end, they would not reach a conclusion. *George Bernard Shaw*

□ I am most fond of talking and thinking; that is to say, talking first and thinking afterward. *Osbert Sitwell*

□ He is every other inch a gentleman. *Rebecca West*

□ Duty is what one expects from others. *Oscar Wilde*

◻ A radical is a man with both feet firmly planted in the air.

*Franklin Delano Roosevelt*

◻ Give me the young man who has brains enough to make a fool of himself. *Robert Louis Stevenson*

◻ There is nothing more certain than that age and youth are right, except perhaps that both are wrong. *Robert Louis Stevenson*

◻ His studies were pursued but never effectually overtaken.

*Herbert George Wells*

◻ A cynic is a man who knows the price of everything and the value of nothing. *Oscar Wilde*

◻ Youth today must be strong, unafraid, and a better taxpayer than its father. *Harry V. Wade*

◻ I am saddest when I sing; so are those who hear me; they are sadder even than I am. *Artemus Ward*

◻ One of the best things in the world is to be a boy; it requires no experience, but needs some practice to be a good one.

*Charles Dudley Warner*

◻ Repartee is something we think of twenty-four hours too late.

*Mark Twain*

◻ Many of us spend half our time wishing for things we could have if we didn't spend half our time wishing.

*Alexander Woollcott*

□ Experience is simply the name we give our mistakes.

*Oscar Wilde*

□ He knew the precise psychological moment when to say nothing.

*Oscar Wilde*

□ He was always late on principle, his principle being that punctuality is the thief of time.

*Oscar Wilde*

□ In examinations the foolish ask questions that the wise cannot answer.

*Oscar Wilde*

□ It is always a silly thing to give advice, but to give good advice is absolutely fatal.

*Oscar Wilde*

□ The old believe everything, the middle-aged suspect everything, the young know everything.

*Oscar Wilde*

□ It was one of those parties where you cough twice before you speak and then decide not to say it after all.

*Pelham Grenville Wodehouse*

□ If you keep your mouth shut you will never put your foot in it.

*Austin O'Malley*

□ Revenge is often like biting a dog because the dog bit you.

*Austin O'Malley*

□ I like work; it fascinates me. I can sit and look at it for hours. I love to keep it by me; the idea of getting rid of it nearly breaks my heart.

*Jerome K. Jerome*

◻ Those that think it permissible to tell white lies soon grow colorblind. *Austin O'Malley*

◻ We go on fancying that each man is thinking of us, but he is not; he is like us; he is thinking of himself. *Charles Reade*

◻ Tell the truth, and so puzzle and confound your adversaries. *Henry Wotton*

◻ Youth calls to youth—and keeps the telephone tied up.

◻ It never occurs to a youth that he will someday know as little as his father.

◻ There has been little real progress in the last six thousand years of history. It took Noah forty years to find a parking space.

◻ Children are creatures that disgrace you in public by behaving just like you do at home.

◻ No opportunity is ever lost. The other person takes those you miss.

◻ Prejudice is a great time-saver for a lot of us: It lets us form solid opinions without bothering to obtain any of the facts.

◻ Sign outside newly painted shopfront in Covent Garden, London: "Wet laqer—lacker—laquar—PAINT."

◻ Everytime you turn green with envy, you are ripe for trouble.

◻ The trouble with people these days is that they want to reach the promised land without going through the wilderness.

◻ A cynic is a man who is never happy unless he is unhappy.

◻ The good years—when the kids are old enough to cut the grass and too young to drive the car.

◻ Inflation is when, after you get the money to buy something, it isn't enough.

◻ An egotist is a person more interested in himself than in me.

◻ Optimist: A cheerful guy who is blissfully unaware of what is going to happen to him.

◻ Don't you just hate to take advice from somebody who needs it himself?

◻ Most of us know how to say nothing—few of us know when.

◻ If there's anything we can't stand it's people who talk while we're interrupting.

◻ You can lead a man up to the university, but you can't make him think.                                     *Finley Peter Dunne*

◻ If the safety pin had been invented this year, instead of long ago, it would probably have six moving parts and two transistors, and require a serviceman twice a year.

◻ Conscience is a smaller inner voice that doesn't speak your language.

◻ After a broken engagement, the young lady returned all of her suitor's letters marked "Fourth Class Male."

◻ A philosopher is a person who says he doesn't care what side his bread is buttered on because he eats both sides anyway.

◻ An optimist is a guy who tells you to cheer up when things are going his way.

◻ Teen-ager placing battery in a radio: "I'm doing a transistor transplant."

◻ Written exams are not what I'm best in; I think of the answers after handing the test in.

◻ The boy who got a wristwatch when he graduated from high school now has a son who wears one to kindergarten.

◻ An after dinner speaker is often a man who rises to the occasion and then stands too long.

◻ Do not suffer from the delusion that you can make your speech immortal by making it everlasting.

◻ A diet is something that takes the starch out of you.

◻ Four years at college and whom has it got me.          *Coed*

□ The best after-dinner speech is one which proves shorter than anyone had ever dared to hope.

□ Some students drink deeply at the fountain of knowledge— others only gargle.

□ Education replaces cocksure ignorance with thoughtful uncertainty.

□ To a parent, a miracle drug is medicine the kids will take without screaming.

□ I want $20,000 to $25,000 starting salary and a shot at the presidency before I'm thirty years of age.          *A Job Applicant*

□ A father has been described as a parent who owns a wallet in which his children's pictures are used as a substitute for money.

□ A bit of inferiority complex could actually improve some people.

□ There is nothing wrong with having nothing to say—unless you insist on saying it.

□ If a cluttered desk is a sign of a cluttered mind, one can't help wondering what an empty desk indicates.

> □ The next time you're discouraged
> and feeling mighty blue,
> Take a look at the mighty oak,
> and see what a nut can do.

☐ Academic is sometimes called a synonym for irrelevant.

*Paul W. McCracken*

☐ You should have quit when you were behind. *James Reston*

☐ Radar spelled backwards is radar; they've got you coming and going. *Denmark Press*

☐ It's time to go on a diet when you sit on one end of a bench and the person on the other end is catapulted into the air.

☐ There are three kinds of boys: the intelligent, the handsome, and the majority.

☐ Modern boy to his teacher, before an exam: "Where can I plug in my electric eraser?"

☐ To err is human—to really foul things up requires a computer.

☐ A sign in the gift shop read: "For the man who has everything; a calendar to remind him when the payments are due."

☐ You can always spot a well-informed man. His views are the same as yours.

☐ Remember—these are the good old days you'll miss in 1990.

☐ A kangaroo went to his psychiatrist and complained, "I'm not feeling jumpy."

□ If those space scientists are so smart, why do they all count backwards?

□ Always put off until tomorrow what you are going to make a mess of today.

□ There's nothing wrong with the younger generation that being a parent and taxpayer won't cure.

□ There are two ways of meeting difficulties; you alter the difficulties, or you alter yourself to meet them.     *Phyllis Bottome*

□ A dog teaches a man fidelity, perserverance, and to turn around two or three times before he gets into bed.     *Robert Benchley*

□ There is nothing like a dish towel for wiping the contented look off a teen-ager's face.

# Part Two

---

## UNUSUAL EXCERPTS FROM BACCALAUREATE, COMMENCEMENT, AND OTHER ADDRESSES

# Patriotism

◻ Pollution is a subject of some concern nowadays. This morning I would like to suggest that the pollution which may well be our greatest curse, even a greater threat to the survival of mankind than the slowly spreading contamination of air, water, and food, is the pollution of ideals. A man without aspirations is not a whole man. A society without a shared and cherished vision of what might be is a desolate society, and one lacking in vitality and cohesiveness.

In the Godkin Lectures at Harvard University last March, John Gardner asserted, "A high level of morale is essential if a society is to succeed in the arduous tasks of renewal." A high level of morale is exactly what we do not have in the United States. It will be my endeavor to examine some possible causes and consequences of this phenomenon and suggest that we begin the difficult decontamination process which will enable our ideals to be revitalized and our humanity to be restored.

Some time back, an African student attending Rockford College spoke to a group on our campus. In the question period which followed, he was asked about his long-range plans. He replied that he wanted to get the best possible education so he could return to serve his people and his country. He said this with vigor and pride and conviction. A glance around the room showed admiration and approval on the part of everyone who heard this testimonial of commitment.

Compare, if you will, the probable reaction that the academic community would give to an American student who asserted that his great life's hope was one of patriotism, that he wanted to devote himself to serving his country and his people. It's a contrast. I suspect that a large portion of intellectual America would be at the very least, embarrassed by such an outburst of patriotic sentiment, if not actually frightened by the fervor of such "un-enlightened insularity." Love of country, that is our country, is now passé, or gauche, or intolerable in much of academia.

Let us try another comparison. As our Negro population reaches for its full and legitimate place in our society, there is a general recognition that one of the necessary ingredients in this fulfilling process is the development of self-esteem. And to this end, there has been a burgeoning of college courses and books and poems and plays and essays on Black culture and Black history and Black biography, so that Black People may be encouraged to take pride in their heritage. How many of the spokesmen who support this logical line of reasoning will accept the same logic when it is applied to the American student, black and white? It seems as if the study of the American heritage is regarded by a growing body of intellectuals to be just as distasteful as the study of Black heritage is regarded to be desirable.

What is this? A double standard? A mindless confusion? Why is patriotism a glory when it operates in a developing nation which may be plagued with gross inequities and bloody struggles for power, and patriotism in an advanced nation a source of indiffer-ence, scorn, or alarm? Why are self-esteem and pride in one's heritage considered beneficial for Blacks and deleterious for other kinds of groupings? I do not claim to know, but I am certain that these apparent double standards which are applied to some of man's motives need to be examined, and worried over and thought through.

*Opening Convocation Address
by President John A. Howard
at Rockford College*

# Not Easy

□ It is a heart-warming experience to see so many of you here and ample testimony of your devotion to the school and your faith in its future. When I was first asked to speak to you on this occasion it seemed like a relatively simple matter, but in the presence of such a distinguished panel I am reminded of the story Bennet Cerf tells of the time when a man asked Billy Rose if he would like to see him dive into a barrel of water from a thousand feet. Billy

Rose said he certainly would, and next day he had his workmen set up a thousand-foot ladder. Mr. Rose held his breath while the man climbed to the top, and stared fascinated as he took a flying leap and landed, splash, in the barrel of water.

"Magnificent," said Billy Rose, "I'll hire you for a hundred a week."

"No," said the man.

"Two fifty a week," said Billy Rose.

"No," said the man.

"You drive a hard bargain," said Billy Rose, "but your act is worth it. Let's not count the pennies. I'll hire you for a thousand a week."

"No," said the man.

"Say, fellow," said Billy Rose, "how much do you want to dive into that barrel?"

"Nothing," said the man. "This is the first time I ever did it, and I don't like it."

Well, in my case, it isn't that I don't like it, but a thousand feet is a lot higher than I thought it was! *Francis O. Grubbs*

# Our Problems

□ The conflicting issues confronting the modern-day businessman may tempt him to quote America's favorite philosopher, Charles Brown. Charlie observed that " . . . no problem facing our nation is so awesome, so complicated or so fraught with danger . . . that the average citizen . . . can't run away from it."

We laugh at Charlie. But he shakes us up, too.

It would be easier if we could say that the problems of the world are for somebody else to solve. But we know that this can't be. *Augustine R. Marosi*

# Creative Thinking

□ A great industrialist, Benjamin Fairless, commented wryly that with our new automation, detail work may well disappear into the innards of a computer. But he added: "If the apple which fell on Sir Isaac Newton's head had happened to fall on a Univac, the machine might have blown a tube ... but it never would have come up with the law of gravity." No, machines will not do our thinking. For that job, we need people who are essentially creative. And the place we are most likely to find them is on the campuses of our colleges.

*From a Commencement Address*
*by G. Keith Funston,*
*former president, New York Stock Exchange*

# Dedication and Hope

☐ The example of Israel is nowhere more vivid than in the field of education. You have the privilege of being graduated today from one of the great universities of the world. But what impresses the world is not so much your fine educational facilities or the magnificence of Mount Scopus where you began to build this university, but the fact that education in Israel permeates the very existence of her people.

You do not "go to school" in Israel; in a sense, this whole land—every home, factory, kibbutz, or even army camp—is a school. Education is an exciting part of life. The mistake that others sometimes make, and that I trust you will never make, is to treat education as a chore instead of a joy; to treat education as an end of education rather than as a beginning.

You consider yourselves pioneers in many things, and rightly so, but I suggest that there is a discovery you are making that you may not be aware of: That a passion for learning diffused throughout a society is the surest road to the achievement of its ideals.

The president of the United States likes to say: "When you're through learning, you're through." And he's right—the strength of a nation, like the strength of an individual, depends on its ability to learn how to change and to grow.

Perhaps the greatest thing that can be said about the people of Israel is that in fighting for the life of your nation, you have stimulated the life of the mind.

42

Today I have been speaking of three discoveries that are being made in the world, and of your part in them in the years ahead.

In creating a lasting prosperity, the human element is at last being recognized as of fundamental importance.

In exercising power in the world, the power of moral example can be far greater than material riches or equipment.

In achieving ideals, a reverence for learning and education is indispensable.

As you take leave of the university, as you graduate into a new life of the mind, may each of you ask yourself this: What am I doing to increase the sum of hope in this world? What am I doing to nourish the sense of purpose that founded this nation and made it strong? What am I doing to teach someone else what I have learned?

In asking questions like these, you will come to new discoveries, you will rise to new challenges, and you will justify the faith of your fathers and the admiration of millions of free men all around the world.

I am deeply honored to join the fellowship of this graduating class and I salute you: Shalom.

*Dr. Arthur Burns,*
*Chairman of the Board of Governors*
*of the Federal Reserve System,*
*giving the Commencement Address*
*at Hebrew University, Jerusalem*

# Morality

□ Some years ago, when Bud Wilkinson had those great national championship teams out in Oklahoma, toward the close of the season he took one of those great teams to play a very mediocre Texas-Christian team. That day, TCU rose to the heights as sometimes a beaten team will. In the closing seconds a receiver dived into the end zone to make a shoestring catch of what would have been the winning touchdown against the national champions. There was a huge upset in view. The crowd was going wild. But down in the end zone the kid stood up . . . walked over to the referee, and said: "No sir, it touched the ground before I caught it."

Now, what was your reaction? Was your first reaction . . . Now wait a minute—that's going too far? The referee didn't see it! He should have kept his mouth shut! Or, should he?

Someday, he may represent you in a statehouse, or in Congress, or in the White House. And what then? Do you want him to keep his mouth shut if no one is looking? Do you want him to base his decisions on political expediency? Or, do you want him to base those decisions on the same kind of inner moral conviction that made him tell the truth to the referee without being asked?

And, who will teach them—by word and deed—that kind of morality if it isn't us? *Ronald Reagan*

# The Supremacy of Logic

□ Ours is an era of sham and pretense, and our public life and even our universities, including this one, are not free from these evils. Both in defense of existing institutions and in pleas for their change or destruction, there has come to be a reliance on spirited exhortation rather than reason, on calls to arms rather than calm marshaling of evidence. It is our task—yours and mine and that of all universities—to help restore the supremacy of logic and to insure freedom from coercion.

*Dean Sidney Davidson*
*of the University of Chicago*
*to a university graduating class,*
*December, 1970*

# What Did You Make of It?

□ I am quite aware that of all occasions when people are impatient with a speaker it is on Commencement Day, and that here above all others the speaker should hold to the three-fold rule of all good public speakers to "Be Heard; Be Brief; and Be Gone!"

Whatever else might be said about the world into which the

graduates of today are stepping, I think it can correctly be said it is one of opportunity. It is indeed one of risk and uncertainty; it is one of stiff competition and heavy demands but withal one of significant rewards and large returns. No one can foretell today what it will make of you. Around the corner lies amazing fortune for some, for others unbelievable discouragement. Fame and success will come to some of you, others of you in spite of everything you can do will not fare so well.

But for all there is opportunity ahead. This is truly an amazing world. It is full of wonderful things but it is so unfinished. We call it a scientific age, yet if one reads in science at all it seems that we must be standing just on the verge of major discoveries. We call it the age of One World, yet the cleavages between nations and races are profound and deep seated and we are a long sea mile from living in this One World in anything like peace and goodwill. We call this an age of prosperity, and it is in so many ways, yet millions of our fellow human beings live in poverty with the basic needs of food, clothing, health and housing still unmet. Your world, as your fathers' before you, is an unfinished world, a world of unlimited opportunity that wants you, needs you—your minds, your hands, and your hearts. . . .

I offer a glimpse of some things I have found in my life as valuable; coins we may use in the market place as we seek life's highest rewards and bargain for life's finest opportunities.

The first of these is the power to **think**. Much is said in commencement addresses about freedom and individuality. But there can be no freedom for you nor can you be much of an individual in this world unless you carry with you wherever you go the willingness to **think** and think hard. . . .

**Thinking** is not something confined to a library, a laboratory, a classroom, or an examination. Thinking goes with living. Learn to think for yourselves, use the powers given you to reason through the issues of life, to make your own choices and decisions, to put your own evaluation upon life's opportunities and life's problems. . . .

Then, too, there is in that little word *work* suggestions of what you can exchange for much that is good.

How easy comes the answer to the question, what does it take to get ahead in life? You know the frequent answer to this question: Know the right people; be at the right place at the right time; having a high I.Q.; pick off the honors at graduation; choose the right parents; get started in the right company.

Yes, these matters do have a bearing on life. But you and I in our rush for success, in our hurry to get ahead, put too much confidence in these things and too little in the importance of being willing to work hard and endlessly.

"Talent? Ability? These are almost beside the point," says one of the business leaders of America about a man's future. "Work," he adds, "is the principal factor!"

Not "what can I get" but "what I can do" ought to predominate your thinking as you set your goals in life.

You may not believe it now but one of your priceless possessions is your power to work. You will know that some day if, after holding a job, you suddenly find yourself unemployed; or if after working hard for many years you suddenly find yourself for reasons of age or health unable to work any longer.

A vice-president of the Aluminum Company of America said to me not long ago when we were talking about the fact that he was not in the habit of taking long vacations, "I enjoy my work!"

That is the spirit life will generously and richly reward. He who finds pleasure in life finds pleasure in work. Industriousness can make the dullest job worthwhile, and he who is industrious and hard working in everything he tackles, whether it is his books, his recreation, his first job, or his life's calling, will find life paying him back many times over.

In Edwin Markham's *Parable of the Builders* we have the story of a certain rich man who had it in his heart to do good. He sent for his carpenter and put before him plans to build a beautiful house on one of the finest locations of his estate. When the plans were laid and the contract decided the rich man went away on a long journey leaving the job with the carpenter. When he had gone the carpenter said to himself, "This is my chance." So he used poor materials and gave poor workmanship that he might have a larger reward for himself for less work. At length the house was finished. The rich man returned and the carpenter brought him the keys. "The house is finished," he said. "Good," said the rich man, "I am glad it is finished. I hope it is well built for all along I have intended to give it to you. The house is yours, you keep the keys." The builder was heartsick. He had only cheated himself, what he had stolen from another was in truth his own.

Each of us builds his own house. To cheat another is to shortchange ourselves. The capacity each of us has for work is a rich and multiplying endowment. Spend it well and lavishly, never counting the cost, and out of this discipline will come amazing rewards from the talents and abilities which are yours and the opportunities which will come your way.

Also, may I suggest you carry with you the quality of perseverance, the willingness to stick to it, to see life through.

I know you think it is important where you are going now that you are through high school. That is indeed important and I trust each of you has thought about it well. But more important than where you go is what you take with you. The attitude you have toward life is of greater consequence for your future than where you are headed immediately. Your willingness to face up to the hard places, to stick to wise decisions, to hold fast to sound ideals and principles, these are the things that will count as life goes on.

In this world of highways and byroads, with circles, overpasses, and cutoffs to reckon with, any driver may get off the route. A driver ought never to be blamed for getting off the road. But for anyone to run out of gas in this modern world, that seems to me to be almost inexcusable. With filling stations on every corner and cars with gas-registering equipment on every dashboard no one except in the severest sort of emergency should run out of fuel.

So in life no one of us can be called to account for getting off the trail somewhat, or making a bad turn next week or next year and having to reverse ourselves, or come back to some starting point and get headed in the right direction. But to run out of gas, to steam up over some dream, some ideal, some hope, some ambition and then peter out, lose interest, get to the place where we don't care any more, that's fatal and I believe well nigh inexcusable. . . .

Not where you go, not what happens to you tomorrow, favorable or unfavorable; not the breaks you get, or those that fail to come your way, these are not the determining factors in life, but the faith you have in yourself; the willingness which you possess to persevere with your ideals, your hopes and your dreams.

We need the *ability to think*, the *willingness to work*, the *quality of perseverance;* and one more, the *power of faith*.

A young man returning from the last war wrote in his diary three vows which he wanted to serve as guides for his life as he came home. The first was this: To maintain steadfastly and at all costs his spiritual disciplines. Second, to keep alive whatever creative powers God had given him. Third, to keep bitterness and resentment out of his life.

A decade later, having earned fame in his particular calling, he says, "I immediately made this discovery. If I kept my first vow I had no trouble with the other two. If I maintained through the exercise of spiritual disciplines touch with God I had little trouble with the other aims of my life."

Come to your world, my young friends, with God as the center of your faith, and the problems you shall face along the way will have a tendency to resolve themselves. As a noted writer of our time said, "Religion is the first thing and the last in a man's life, and until a man finds God he begins at no beginning and works to no end."

The coin which in the market place we can use in exchange for life's greatest and most enduring rewards is experience with and knowledge of God. To live with God is to understand ourselves better, each other, and the universe of which we are a part.

When at the end of our course in life we are asked, **What did you make of it?** more will be implied than **what did you make** on the average in your annual salary. He who along his way of life will reach up to God will find God reaching down to him.

Life, dear friends, was made for living. Each of us through the door of graduation goes out into a world of his own. We can't go home again, and what our port of call eventually will be no one now can say.

I challenge you on your commencement day not only to hitch your wagon to a star, but to link your soul in unremitting faith to the sure foundation of the divine will, in whose love "all things can work together for good."

May I close by paraphrasing something the Archbishop of Canterbury said to the principals at a prominent wedding some years ago:

"We all wish you happiness, but our wishes cannot give it. Nor can it come from outward circumstances. It can come only from yourselves, from the spirit that is within you. You cannot choose what changes and chances are to befall you in the coming years, but you can choose to meet them with scrip that will be acceptable at any and all points of exchange; the ability to think; the willingness to work; the quality of perseverance; and the power of faith."

May these attend you, and may God bless you all along the way.

*Excerpts from a high school commencement address
by the Reverend W. Ralph Ward, Jr.*

# Converting Liabilities into Assets

□ I have chosen as my subject "Converting Liabilities into Assets." I think I can state my theme in the form of a paradox. The greatest asset is to have a liability. The greatest liability is to have no liability. A very interesting book appeared some time ago written by eleven psychiatrists who had locked themselves up together in a hotel for about a week to discuss a very important problem, "Why Men Fail." They came out with a dozen conclusions—some four or five of which I'll share with you this evening. The first is, that the majority of people who succeed in life are not more gifted than those who fail. Second: the majority of those who fail in life are not less gifted than those who succeed. Third: the majority of people go all through life using less than 40 percent of their God-given abilities. Fourth: the majority of people who have handicaps, liabilities, and frustrations, who are crippled or blind or deaf, who have every reason to fail, now mark you, the majority who have every reason to fail—fail to fail. They make good. . . .

What about the handicaps? I am thinking for the moment of a man named Whistler. The great ambition of his life was to be a soldier. He got an appointment and he went to West Point. At the end of the first year, he "flunked" his chemistry. He was allowed to come back, and the next year he flunked his chemistry again and they had to drop him. He went back home. When such things happen to them, some people lose their courage in life, they feel they are no good, they are "washed out," they're done. He began scratching in the sand and he found that he could draw things. Then he began taking up colors and found out that he could mix colors and paint. I needn't tell you that Whistler became one of the great artists of all times. Now some of you are going to tell me

49

he achieved fame in spite of his handicap and I say to you, because of his handicap.

Take an oyster. From an evolutionary point of view, it is a mollusk; it is way down in the evolutionary scale by millions of years. When a grain of sand gets into an oyster, it has a liability and it wiggles attempting to expel the liability. An oyster has a brain one millionth as big as a pin head. Instinct causes it to wiggle out the grain of sand. It usually succeeds. But when it fails to get rid of a liability like a grain of sand, it clamps down, closes up, and converts that liability into a precious pearl. Converting liabilities into assets! Handicaps.

A long way back there was a man named Demosthenes. You remember him? Demosthenes couldn't speak. When he dreamed, he dreamed of a mighty audience in front of him, and in his dream felt that by the sheer inflection of his voice he could make strong men cry one moment and laugh the next. Then he awakened and found that it was not a dream but a nightmare—he couldn't talk. It was before the day of apartment houses and yet the neighbors found fault with the noises that he made when he tried to speak. So Demosthenes went down to the seashore where there were no people. He saw pebbles lying on the shore and the strange idea came to him—he didn't have enough liabilities! He felt that if he just filled up his mouth with pebbles and, if he could talk just as well with a mouth full of pebbles—he couldn't talk worse—maybe by removing one of the pebbles each week, he would learn how to speak. Need I tell you that Demosthenes became not one of the greatest, but in all likelihood, the greatest orator of all time?

Think for a moment of John Bunyan. He lived two hundred years ago in England. His religious and theological views were unconventional and because of the moral climate of the day he was thrust into prison. He was a tinker, a mender of pots and pans, and he left behind a wife and four daughters, one of whom was stone blind. They put him in Bedford jail for seven years where he had only dry bread for food, dirty water for drink, and a stone for a pillow. He certainly had enough alibies if he wanted an alibi. But something happened to him, the humble tinker became a great thinker and in the alchemy of his spirit it was transformed and transfused and transfigured into spiritual assets. He wrote *The Pilgrim's Progress*, one of the great religious classics of all times. In spite of his difficulties? Nay, because of his difficulties.

50

Some years ago I was asked to give a commencement address at one of the great western universities. The president of the university and I stood and watched the graduates as they marched in. As we stood there the president said to me: "Oh, if you could only have been here two years ago. What a great commencement we had." I said, "Did you have a good speaker that year?" He said, "Oh, something happened, I wish you could have witnessed it; I could hardly believe what I saw." And I asked, "Just what was it?" Said he, "Four years earlier a little clump of flesh that called himself a student came to us; we didn't know whether to take him or not. The first week the professor of English said, 'When I call your name, rise, and after that I'll know you by name.' A name was called and no one rose; it was called a second time and still no one arose. The professor became just a bit indignant and said, 'Didn't I ask you to rise?' A voice chirped back, 'I'm sorry, sir, I haven't stood on my feet since I was two years old.' The four years passed and that little clump of flesh had won every honor that the university had ever bestowed. When the football captain had got his diploma, people applauded; when the Phi Beta Kappas got their diplomas, nobody applauded; then a name was called, and the football captain and the baseball captain made a basket out of their arms and they took this little clump of humanity and carried him across the stage." Then the president said to me, "The applause was so deafening that the walls began to tremble and the chandeliers began to swing. Mr. Mann, I have never witnessed anything like that in all my life." It isn't what happens to us, it's what happens within us that really counts.

Some of you may remember my "friend" Socrates. He had a great liability. He had "matrimonial indigestion." Do you know what that is? His wife didn't agree with him. She nagged and nagged and nagged, till she got tired of nagging and then she scolded till she got tired of scolding and then she started to nag all over again. Some men go out and get drunk and others jump into the river under such conditions. Socrates went out on the street. He couldn't even get a "thin" word in "edgewise" at home and so he talked to everybody on the street. When a man said, "Socrates, it's a nice day," he asked, "What do you mean by 'a nice day.' If it were this way every day, we'd all starve to death. The umbrella man would go broke." Then he would go to another man and finally they accused him of being the brightest man in the whole

51

community and he said, "I plead guilty. I'm the brightest man that ever lived. I know that I know nothing and I've met no one that knows that much." Convert liabilities into assets!

I close with this illustration. A little boy lived in Edinburgh. He had trouble with his leg, so he went to the doctor. The doctor said he couldn't help him and that there was only one doctor who could and he lived in London. It was before the days of the "rule of thumb"—hitch-hiking. So he rode on the train part of the way, he tried to walk on his poor leg part of the way, and in the last stretch he crawled on his stomach like a worm. The doctor saw him and said that one of his legs would have to be amputated immediately, but that he would try to save the other. He lay on a bed week after week and month after month without a smile from anyone save from those angels in white, sometimes called "nurses." Then a great day came, there was to be an international meeting of great physicians. Twelve world specialists were brought in to examine him, to see if they could save that other leg. While they were out in consultation, he reached over to one of the beds and got a stub of a pencil and then reached out to another bed and got a piece of wrapping paper and there wrote these lines. The moment I begin them, you will know that I am talking of the "Invictus" by William Ernest Henley:

> Out of the night that covers me,
> Dark as a pit from pole to pole,
> I thank whatever gods there be,
> For my unconquerable soul.
> In a fell clutch of circumstance,
> I have not winced or cried aloud,
> Under the bludgeonings of chance,
> My head is bloody but unbowed.
> Beyond this place of wrath and tears
> Looms but the horror of the shade
> And yet the menace of the years
> Finds, and shall find, me unafraid.
> It matters not how straight the gate
> How charged with punishment the scroll,
> I am the master of my fate
> I am the captain of my soul.

"Invictus." Unconquerable, insuperable, indomitable. Not what happens to us, but in the divine alchemy of the spirit transfused, transformed, transfigured, what happens within us. Invictus—unconquerable!

*Excerpts from an address*
*by Dr. Louis L. Mann*

# A Time of Ambitions and Dreams

□ I know that graduation is a very happy time, a time of great ambitions and wonderful dreams. My purpose in emphasizing today some of the more serious aspects of the meaning of graduation was not to sound a jarring note. I had no intention of cooling your ambitions or of dispelling your wonderful dreams. Rather, I urge you to cling to your ambitions and your dreams. It is because I have hope for your ambitions, and because I believe in your dreams that I wanted to tell you how I think you can best make your dreams come true, and, especially, that dream that I am sure that you and I and all of us have of seeing America, our beloved country, lead the world to peace.

Off in the southern part of France, there is a beautiful medieval city called Carcassonne. Its thick granite walls, its broad moat, the drawbridges, its crenelated embattlements and lofty towers, its waving flags and crooked old streets and ancient houses make of it a kind of a dream city, transplanted from a far-off past into our own day. Once upon a time, there was a traveler whose dream it was to walk to Carcassonne. As he made his way along the road, he came upon a peasant. "How far is it," he said, "to Carcassonne?" "How far is it to Carcassonne," replied the peasant; "Sir, that I do not know. But that this is the road to Carcassonne of that I am sure. For those who return says that at the end lies beautiful Carcassonne."

Were you graduates to ask me today, "How far is it to the city of your dreams and ambitions; how far is it to the Carcassonne of that glorious dream that you and all of us have of seeing America lead the world to peace?" I should have to answer, like the French peasant, "How far is it to the Carcassonne of your dreams? That

I do not know. But this I do know. That as long as you remain on the road pointed out to you during your happy days at the College of New Rochelle, you are on the right road. And your best dreams for yourselves and for America will come true." On the journey to the Carcassonne of those dreams, may God be with you. . . .

*From a commencement address*
*by Edward B. Rooney, S.J.,*
*Director, Jesuit Educational Association*

# Your Values

□ I'm genuinely pleased to share with you these important moments in your lives. I'm pleased, first of all, because this ceremony of commencement represents a celebration of one of the most cherished cultural values of the human race—enlightenment. I'm pleased, secondly, because this ceremony represents for us all an occasion for sober reflection on the deeper meanings of life. And it is to this purpose that I wish to invite your attention for a few moments this morning.

You shall live out your lives in the most sophisticated culture ever to have been developed on the planet Earth. It is at once your high privilege and your awesome burden to bear the label "Twentieth-Century Man." Your age is an age of "Adventures of the Mind," especially as such adventure is reflected in scientific endeavor. Your age is the age of the atom, of space travel, of the thinking machine, of drugs that can shape men's minds, of symbolic logic, of hidden persuaders, of assault on the very riddle of life itself. Your age is hardly, however, an age of "Adventures of the Spirit." Twentieth-century man celebrates his mentality but not his humanity. He strives to shove out his mental horizons, but neglects to cultivate the humane side of his nature.

The real question of the future, it appears to me, is the question of whether man can learn to educate his heart as well as his head—whether he can learn to combine mentality with morality. Loren Eiseley, an American anthropologist, has recently put the issue with impressive clarity: "A future worth contemplating will not be achieved solely by flights to the far side of the moon. It will not be found in space. It will be achieved, if it is achieved at all, only in our individual hearts."

Here is the overriding issue that I wish to explore with you—the issue of creating a better moral world for yourselves and your contemporaries. It must be obvious that whether you will find for yourselves the so-called Good Life and whether you will be able to help build a Good Society will rest at last on the question of your vision of the good. You shall need to take stock of your values, and find for yourselves a firm moral stance.

*From a high school commencement address*
*by Dr. Ralph Eubanks*

# Happiness

□ My mind goes back today over other days, other milestones, other graduations reminiscent of this one. Two years ago, I was invited to make the commencement address at a preparatory school in Connecticut. I found it somewhat dispiriting to have to tell the graduates, on that lovely spring day, that when I recalled my own graduation X years before, I could not remember the name, the face nor a trace of the remarks made by the commencement speaker of the day. His mark upon my memory was as unblemished as I am sure mine will be upon yours some years hence.

Therefore knowing that this message may be soon forgotten, I feel I can speak with candor and thus speak more boldly particularly since I am now no longer a member of our national government. . . .

A final word about being both useful and enjoying life. "Happiness," said John F. Kennedy, "is self-fulfillment along lines of excellence." Self-fulfillment is a marvelous word, rich with many superb connotations, all susceptible here at this great university to a wide variety of translations into actuality.

And so, in the spirit of this splendid movement, warm with goodwill and the fellowship of the future, I say with a full heart—go forth and fulfill yourself.

*Angier Biddle Duke, Former Ambassador*

# An Educated Person

☐ Far too many of us are content with what others consider adequate. In fact, we have an almost frenetic resistance to anything that would set us apart from others. The old lady in Oklahoma was not too far out of character in declaring, "I ain't no better than anybody else but I'm jest ez good." Certainly we should all aspire toward something more than the ordinary. We should achieve more than the average.... It is indeed fitting, therefore, that recognition in the form of this Honors Convocation be given to excellence and that certain ones be singled out for having placed the superior above the commonplace and distinction above mediocrity.

On this occasion I would like to talk on the theme "On Being an Educated Person." Throughout the ages philosophers and writers have reflected on what constitutes an educated person. Some have taken a cynical view. Thus Pascal, seventeenth-century French philosopher and mathematician, defined an educated person as "one who has substituted learned ignorance for natural ignorance." This skepticism was shared by John Jay Chapman who expressed his view in this way:

"I hate the young. I am worn out with them. They absorb you and suck you dry and are vampires and selfish brutes at best. Give me some good old rain-soaked clubmen who can't be improved and make no moral claims and let me play checkers with them and look out of the club window and think what I will have for dinner."

Others, however, have expressed their views in a more constructive vein. A former distingushed professor on the faculty of the University of Wisconsin, once defined an educated person as one "who tries to understand the whole of knowledge as well as one man can." Mark van Doren held that the purpose of education is to see that "each man becomes more than he is," while William Whewell thought of education as the means "to connect a man's mind with the general mind of the human race."

... Yet while more and more people have been educated we seem to be living more precariously than ever before. We are uncertain of ourselves. ...

Certainly a reduction in illiteracy has not resulted in our devising a more intelligent way of living. For if a close correlation had existed between literacy and intelligence, then we should have witnessed in recent years a decline in war, civil strife, crime, delinquency, and general social maladjustment. Yet quite the reverse is true, for this highly literate twentieth century of ours has also turned out to be the bloodiest and most turbulent in the history of mankind. Thus we find ourselves today among the most highly educated people in the world. Yet at the same time we seem incompetent to deal with the immediate problems at hand. Technologically we have moved forward at the terrifying speed of a jet-propelled plane but our social behavior is still moving at the slow pace of an oxcart. Our technical competence is superb but we have neglected other competences of equal importance. For many of us the times are like "a tale told by an idiot, full of sound and fury, signifying nothing."

Sometimes it takes an outsider from another era to analyze our problems and present answers. So this morning I would like to take as a point of departure the views of a well-known Chinese philosopher on the matter of being an educated person.

"The men of old," Confucius held, "when they wished their virtues to shine throughout the land, first had to govern their states well. To govern their states well, they first had to establish harmony in their families. To establish harmony in their families they first had to set their minds in order. To set their minds in order, they first had to make their purpose sincere. To make their purpose sincere, they first had to extend their knowledge to the utmost. Such knowledge is acquired through a careful investigation of things. For with things investigated knowledge becomes complete. With knowledge complete the purpose becomes sincere. With the purpose sincere the mind is set in order. With the mind set in order there is a real self-discipline. With real self-discipline the family achieves harmony. With harmony in the family the state becomes well-governed. With the state well-governed there is peace throughout the land."

This Chinese philosopher was emphasizing several fundamental concepts. He contended as basic to an individual's education the extension of knowledge through a careful investigation of things for only in this way could the mind be set in order and a high degree of self-discipline be achieved. Certainly there is great need today for a careful investigation of things and for well-disciplined and self-disciplined minds. Yet this is not always easy to achieve.

For there are some among us who believe that they already have a monopoly of truth and wisdom and are thus intolerant of anyone who would challenge their particular version of the truth. There are others who are continually narrowing the area in which the truth operates so that soon it no longer has any special significance. And then there are those who do not have time or energy to seek the truth. They yield to the temptation of cutting corners, of finding shortcuts. . . .

The Chinese philosopher was not satisfied with just a careful investigation of things. Certainly education has an obligation to send out into the world persons eager for truth and an understanding of how to attain it. Yet the mere search for truth, he contended, would not make of us educated people. Thus he spoke of a sincerity of purpose and a concern over virtue.

Dr. William Harper, president of the University of Chicago, sounded the same keynote in speaking to the entering class of young men in 1903 when he delivered in sixty seconds the following message:

"Young gentlemen, you have come here in the hope of furthering your education. . . . An educated man is a man who by the time he is twenty-five years old has a clear theory, formed in the light of human experience down the ages, of what constitutes a satisfying life, a significant life, and who by the age of thirty has a moral philosophy consonant with human experience. If a man reaches these ages without having arrived at such a theory, such a philosophy, then no matter how many facts he has learned or how many processes he has mastered, that man is an ignoramus and a fool, unhappy, probably dangerous. That is all. Good afternoon."

. . . Do you consider yourself an educated person? I will rest my case with you.

*Dr. J. Martin Klotsche*
*speaking at an Honors Convocation,*
*University of Wisconsin, Milwaukee*

# Where Is the Evidence?

□ One of the more perilous occupations of these exciting times is that of a university president or dean. It was not always so. A dean could once count on a certain number of predictable vocational hazards. He knew that he had to deal with an unreasonable central authority, temperamental faculty, jealous peers, and, occasionally, querulous alumni. But these were familiar concerns, and if he had keen eyesight and was capable of fast footwork he could generally escape mortal damage.

The job has become more hazardous, however, in unfamiliar ways. The silent generation of the 1950s has become the vocal one of the 1960s and 1970s. Students have discovered the power of speech and action; they have found their tongue and are exercising it, with considerable gusto and only occasionally questionable content. This has helped to make an administrator's life more exciting in new and unpredictable ways.

My intention is not to involve you in the concerns of the deanhood but to offer a related admonition that I hope will remain with you after you leave these sheltering walls. If I have a prayer for you in your postuniversity life, it is that you continue to cultivate what we have worked to inculcate—an attitude of benign skepticism about virtually everything—a constant query of "where is the evidence?" in support of ideas and institutions, new and old. . . .

Thus my admonition "seek the evidence" has sprouted a twig, "distinguish fact from opinion." There are many twigs; they have to do with the evaluation and application of evidence. Let me describe them briefly, in the hope that you will recall and employ them.

I hope first of all that you have learned something about the techniques and applications of logic, and that you also have learned that logic is a way of going wrong with confidence.

I hope you also have learned that your senses can perceive the truth—and also can be deceived by illusion.

I hope you have learned that to identify a thing and put a name to it is not the same as understanding it.

I hope you are aware that empirical evidence alone can lead you into error, but also that theory without evidence remains theory alone.

I hope you perceive that certainty is the comfort of the unschooled, and that there is no convincing evidence for its existence.

I hope you have learned that intuition can leap mountains, but more often stumbles on molehills.

I hope you have learned not to be trapped by reliance upon

numbers alone, however important quantitative data have come to be.

I hope you have learned that, as Occam's Razor would have it, the most economical answer is best, but that simple answers are not simply arrived at.

I hope you have learned that truth is provisional and subject to the development of additional evidence. If this were not so, the world would be flat.

I hope you have learned that the walls which separate one field of knowledge from another are highly permeable membranes. . . .

I have admonished you enough for one Convocation. Let me end this discourse with the plea that we not permit this search for evidence to paralyze our activity seeking improvement, to stay our quest for the impossible dream. We are surrounded by conditions about which it is inhuman to remain passive, by issues about which it is inhuman to remain silent. But let us exercise our humanity by seeking answers—in whatever time is available to us by first asking the educated man's query, Where is the evidence?

*Sidney Davidson, Dean of the Graduate School of Business, delivered at the Convocation Address at the 334th Convocation of the University of Chicago.*

# Character, Wealth, and Power

□ And now, before I close, I would like to say a word to the young men and women who this day join the great host of our alumni. Some of you are being awarded your first degrees, which means that you have had a priceless opportunity to broaden your lives by a study of those liberal arts which are a necessary foundation upon which to build successfully any professional specialization. Many of you are now receiving your advanced degrees as a symbol of your proficiency in preparing yourselves for the professional careers of your choice. All of you now belong to Columbia as Columbia belongs to you.

Your education has now been successfully begun. If you ever feel that it is finished, then somehow your Columbia experience has been a failure. An unquenchable thirst for knowledge is one of man's most cherished possessions. Though the individual is born with this desire, formal education provides an organized oppor-

60

tunity to examine the lore of the past and a method and discipline for that most exciting of all activities—the discovery of new truth.

You have been greatly fortunate in that you have had an opportunity to work for a time in this community of scholars. I can ask for you, now as you leave us, no greater wish than that your lives will be rich and rewarding—to yourselves, your associates, and your country. I hope that we have opened new vistas to you. Finally, I hope that we have helped you to realize that character is more important than wealth and power. Even though you have the latter and do not have the former, you will be no credit to this institution. To have integrity . . . "is to be good, great and joyous, beautiful and free; this is alone life, joy, empire, and victory."

Dr. Grayson Kirk speaking at<br>commencement exercises at Columbia University

# A Double Mission

□ Ours is the only society in recorded history that has failed to recognize that education must have a double mission. On the one hand, education should develop new knowledge, transmit knowledge to the young, and sharpen the intellectual tools of the student.

On the other hand, education must try to help the young people develop the attitudes and the pattern of conduct which will enable them to live affirmatively and productively in the world. We have abandoned the latter function.

If one so much as mentions the concept of character education in the professional meeting of higher education, the response is almost always one of derision or at least amazement.

Dr. John A. Howard, President, Rockford College

# Closing Gaps and Building Bridges

□ The month of June approaches,
And soon across the land
The graduation speakers
Will tell us where we stand.

We stand at Armageddon,
In the vanguard of the press;
We're standing at the crossroads,
At the gateway to success.

We stand upon the threshold
Of careers all brightly lit.
In the midst of all this standing,
We sit and sit and sit.

It may be that some of you are praying the prayer that one fellow prayed as he came to church:

Now I lay me down to sleep,
The sermon's long and the subject's deep:
If he gets through before I wake,
Somebody give me a gentle shake!

Or, you may feel like the man who said:

I never see my preacher's eyes,
Regardless of how bright they shine;
For when he prays he closes his,
And when he preaches he closes mine.

Really, I hope it won't be quite that bad for you during these next few moments.

A few days ago a mother sat in my office and said, "Can you do something about my daughter? I simply do not understand her." Shortly afterwards, the daughter sat in the same office and said matter-of-factly, "My mother doesn't love me. She doesn't even care about me."

Two bewildered parents said, "We don't know what went wrong." And a teen-ager said of them, "If what they have is religion, I'd just as soon not have it."

Now, it doesn't take a lot of "smart" to recognize that there is a gap, a glaring gap, in these relationships. Perhaps the expression *generation gap* has been overworked, but it is dramatically descriptive. The truth is, there is a generation gap. There always has been. There always will be. There needs to be. This is written into the growth process of life itself. Young people are not supposed to act or react like adults. And adults make fools out of themselves when they try to act and react like teen-agers.

Now, I am concerned about the "generation gap," and it is a valid concern. But I am even more concerned about some other gaps, some glaring gaps within individual personalities. I am concerned about some gaps in my life and yours that must be narrowed and closed else life will pass us by completely.

Let me be more specific. The average high school graduate has been handed a wealth of information. The accumulation of knowledge has reached staggering proportions. Someone has calculated that the amount of data, facts, and figures, doubles every ten years. For instance, most of the medicines prescribed today were unknown ten years ago. A large percentage of the goods available today were not on the market prior to the dawn of the Space Age. It has also been suggested that if the high school senior of World War I days could be recalled, invited to join your class, required to gather all of the information fed to you, it would take him the rest of his life and he still wouldn't be to first base.

I read a rather provocative and frightening statement the other day. "The next generation may well experience the perfection of the control of man's mind. Experience will be available *on order* to any depth and intensity using chemical, psychological, and physical stimulations." Someone else has said, "Knowledge is emerging as the most important source of power." Now, no one would question the importance of knowledge, but what if there is no wisdom! We are grateful for every new discovery, and with creative minds we shall continue to explore and learn. But there is a glaring gap with some of us that must be closed: the gap between knowledge and wisdom. For you see, knowledge without wisdom is like the spokes of a wheel with no hub to tie them together. The wheel collapses under the weight of the load. It is a frightening thought but knowledge can outrace wisdom. Knowledge has given man the ability to destroy himself. The fundamental question now is, will wisdom give him the ability to live with himself? . . .

The gap between knowledge and wisdom must be closed. There is a second glaring gap: the gap between our dreams and our discipline.

While preparing this particular message the stereo was softly playing in the background.

63

A law was made a distant moon ago here,
July and August cannot be too hot;
And there's a legal limit to the snow here—
In Camelot.

The winter is forbidden 'til December,
And exits March the second on the dot;
By order summer lingers through September—
In Camelot.

The rain may never fall 'til after sundown,
By eight the morning fog must disappear;
In short, there's simply not . . . a more congenial spot
For happily ever aftering than here in Camelot.

Camelot . . . Camelot . . .
I know it gives a person pause,
But in Camelot those are legal laws.

The snow may never slush upon the hillside,
By nine P.M. the moonlight must appear;
In short, there's simply not . . . a more congenial spot
For happily ever aftering than here in Camelot.

Now in one way or another, most of us dream of our Camelots. There's nothing wrong with this if we are willing to narrow the gap between our dreams and the discipline needed to make them become reality.

While I was teaching on the college campus, I had a student who enrolled in one of my courses with a faraway look in his eyes. In fact, his look was so faraway that it seldom landed on the textbook! He talked of his desires, dreams, what he would do, and how much he expected to achieve—for himself. He dreamed and dreamed without any discipline. As I recall, he had a "D" in my class. He nearly flunked out of college. I saw him a few years ago working as an attendant at a service station. An honorable job, mind you, but a far cry from his "Camelot."

We are dreamers. We are idealists. We dream of academic achievements, ideal family relationships, instant success, a better nation, a better world, a more meaningful church, and independence and freedom. But these dreams will fade as "Camelot" unless the gap between the dreams and disciplines is closed.

She is a nurse, a missionary stationed in Paraguay. One day I said to her, "Do you like your work?" She answered, "Like my work? No, I don't like my work. I don't like living in another land, speaking a foreign language, having the wrong color of skin, seeing the flag of another country flying over the compound. Neither do I like the poverty and filth all around me. I don't like leaving my mother alone in the hills of Arkansas. But heaven help us if we only do for God in today's world what we like to do!"

Dreams? Wonderful! But close the gap between dreams and discipline.

Again, if life has any meaning, if we do more than merely exist, if there is to be any satisfaction and achievement and purpose, then the gap between what I am and what I ought to be must be narrowed and closed. Let me ask you some probing questions: Who are you? Where are you? What are you? Six thousand students were recently interviewed. Most of these had some identification with the church. The number one characteristic of these students was alienation. There was alienation from self, others, the world, and God. Each lived on his own isolated island. The conclusion of the interviews indicated the average student is often an alienated individual living apart from honest involvement in the world and never realizing the ultimate purpose for which he was created. Let one young person express it:

> Let the world roll on,
> In all its racket,
> In all its clamor,
> In all its confusion.
>
> Let people beat their heads together,
> In all their ignorance,
> In all their stupidity,
> In all their lack of vision.
>
> Let everything go on around me.
> I don't care.
> I don't need this world.
> It doesn't matter.

I have my life,
My thoughts,
My company,
My companionship.
Who needs anything else?
I'll just sit here quietly and die.

So, here we are. And here some of us are destined to stay. It's like the road sign on the country road before paved highways, "Choose carefully your rut; you'll be in it the next thirty miles." Choose carefully your rut; you'll be in it for the next thirty years . . . unless the gap is narrowed between what you are and what you ought to be! But listen! I have good news! You don't have to live a life of alienation. You don't have to stay where you are. You don't have to spend the next thirty years in a muddy, bogged-down rut. God knows you—all about you. He knows what you are and what you ought to be. He has already made His move to close the gap. Why . . . *He's built a bridge*—from His heart to yours. That bridge is personified in His Son, Jesus Christ. "For God so loved the world that he gave his only begotten Son that whosoever believeth in him should not perish but have everlasting life." And Jesus who came to close the gap between what we are and what we ought to be said, "I am come that you might have life and that you might have it more abundantly." You see, you don't have to stay where you are and you don't have to be forever what you are now. God loves you and He created you for something better than this. He has built His bridge! Cross over it!

Generation gap? Yes. But more important are the gaps within generations: the gap between knowledge and wisdom, the gap between dreams and discipline, the gap between what I am and what I ought to be in the eyes of God. I challenge you today to cross over the bridge that God has built!

*The Reverend Bruce McIver, Dallas, Texas*

# His Lot for All Time

□ I am delighted to take part in this convocation which confirms the assumption of his duties by your new president. He comes to this leadership with experience and knowledge.

66

I might be expected to comment on the courage of a man willing to lose his individuality for the benefit of an institution, and with the confidence to try to solve some of the difficulties of higher education. The title for these remarks, "His Lot for All Times," might be a hint that this celebration witnesses the sentencing of a once free soul to the doom reserved on earth for college administrators. I reject that suggestion, and along with it the frustration, dismay, and pity now fashionable. This is a day for rejoicing. It symbolizes a transcendent cause worthy of great effort. I congratulate President Hotchkiss and Lake Forest College for the opportunity and adventure which lie ahead.

The words which read "His lot, not for an hour, but all time" come from a recent translation of Lucretius. They describe the burden which all men carry.

> Men seem to feel some burden on their souls,
> Some heavy weariness, could they but know
> Its origin, its cause, they'd never live
> The way we see most of them do, each one
> Ignorant of what he wants, except a change,
> Some other place to lay his burden down.
>
> . . . So each man flees
> Himself, or tries to, but of course that pest
> Clings to him all the more ungraciously.
>
> The problem being his lot, not for an hour,
> But for all times . . .

The poet's words leap two thousand years. They remind us that much of the collective and individual burden of mankind is not new. The poem is not a lament. Rather, it is a passionate exaltation of the miraculous powers of reason and understanding. . . .

I do not forget that few institutions, if any, in American life have the importance of our colleges and universities. I am not blind to the fact that they may be in for a difficult period because of pressure of competing needs. There probably has been no time in American history when it was more important for us than now to understand the many cultures of the world, including our own diverse inheritance. The colleges and universities are the major link in that inheritance and to these cultures. They have kept alive that use of reason and understanding which is the answer to the lot of

67

man. The dedication of men and women of good will and wisdom to the preservation of these institutions—this institution—is a cause for rejoicing. We must wish them strength, not for themselves, but for all of us.

*From an address delivered*
*by Edward H. Levi,*
*President of the University of Chicago,*
*at the installation convocation*
*of Dr. Eugene Hotchkiss III,*
*President of Lake Forest College,*
*Lake Forest, Illinois*

# Reflections on a Time of Trouble

□ I ought to tell you at the outset that it is with mixed feelings that I stand here before you today. Not only is it commencement for those of you who sit here before us black-robed, wide-eyed, and anxious, but also for some of the rest of us it is a rather solemn, even painful, reminder of how long it has been since we sat where you now sit. I vaguely remember that when I was in college I regarded with wonder the notion that anyone who has been out as long as I have could still remain vertical. And if you wonder what it's like to be out of college thirty-four years, I can best respond in the words of Lord Clement Atlee, who, as you may know, was asked how it felt to be eighty years of age. "Well," replied Lord Atlee thoughtfully, "considering the alternatives, it feels great!"

. . . In the next sixty seconds, about 200 human beings are going to be born on this earth. Half of them will be dead before they are a year old. About 160 of these human beings now being born will be black, or red, or yellow. Of those who survive past their first year, another half will be dead before they are sixteen. So that means that of the 200 human beings now coming into this earth, about 50 will live past the age of sixteen. And if we focus upon them and multiply by millions and yet billions, we can see the human beings of this earth and here they are. They are going to have an age expectancy of about thirty years, they are going to be hungry and tired and sick most of their lives. Most of them will

68

never learn to read or write. Most of them will spend their lives tilling the soil, working for landlords, living in tents or mud huts. They, as their fathers and their forefathers before them, will lie under the open skies of Asia and Africa and Latin America waiting, watching, hoping. These are the human beings of this earth. These are your brothers and sisters with whom you inherit this time of trouble. . . .

Since the days of President Monroe, no responsible American leader has dared tell us that Latin America can be neglected or ignored. It is our nearest neighbor. It is growing explosively from two hundred and thirty million now to six hundred million by the end of the century; it is a continent in ferment.

As you walk Latin American streets today, you are accompanied everywhere by poverty, and poverty is escorted by its inevitable companion, disease. You see housing which is not housing but hovel. You find vast millions of people either totally or functionally illiterate, and yet that fact seems almost irrelevant. Books, after all, are not edible. Latin America won't go away if we turn our backs on it, nor will its problems. Yet all too many in this country, both in and out of government, have relegated Latin America to the backwash of history. . . .

The average American . . . knows little or nothing about Latin America because the chief characteristic of the average American's attitude toward his neighbors to the South has been ignorance—an ignorance that has been far more our loss than theirs. For knowledge about Latin America and its culture and its people is not just information and legend about a quaint, underdeveloped part of the world; it's an important part of the knowledge of every educated American; about one of the richest and most exciting cultures in the world; and about a continent in the midst of a peaceful revolution. It is the youth of Latin America which will determine whether that revolution now underway there will succeed or fail.

Young people already make up two-thirds of the total population of Latin America and their numbers are growing. They are dissatisfied with conditions and are determined to build a society that will ensure their people the greatest degree of freedom and individual dignity and opportunity. Even as young people everywhere . . . are restless and prone to impatience, they are skeptical of our aims and more willing to blame the Yankee for their problems than to understand the difficulties involved in solving them.

*Excerpts from a commencement address
at the College of Wooster by Sol M. Linowitz (1969).*

# Crisis of Our Age

☐ The fundamental crisis of our age, not unlike that of other ages, is undoubtedly moral and spiritual in character. Without a moral society to recurringly call immoral man to account, we cannot long survive as a democratic Christian society. Our colleges and universities have no alternative to providing more effective learning opportunities for developing moral and social responsibility in the individual. We must develop the moral qualities to control automation and the atom, and for living with the Russians—or our epitaph is written:

> A tear for the world,
> A cosmic erratum;
> Started with Adam
> And ended with Atom.

To preserve and enrich the spiritual values of our civilization does not require any profound changes in the meaning and mission of higher education. The abiding functions of colleges and universities are four:

> to transmit the cultural heritage, enriched;
> to push back the frontiers of knowledge;
> to draw out the latent talents of youth; and
> to make more evident the ends for which we live.

Colleges are strong bastions against ignorance and irrationality. They are testaments to man's perennial struggle to make a better world. They are places of higher yearning as well as of higher learnings.

*From a commencement address
by Ernest V. Hollis*

# The Three Don'ts

□ I do assure my classmates that I intend to speak briefly. You have been sitting on a school bench for sixteen years, perhaps more, and I know you don't want to be kept sitting there much longer.

As a matter of fact one of the greatest men of our time, the late President Eisenhower, once told me something on this subject. "The only virtue that can be presented in a commencement speech," he said, "is brevity."

So with his admonition in mind, I would like to make a deal with today's graduates of Grove City College. I will talk for just about fifteen more minutes, if you will settle back from the takeoff blocks at the edge of your seats into a comfortable position and really listen for that long. In that time, there are just three things I want to say. They are a distillation of all the advice I could conceivably give you.

Don't downgrade the future. You can play any part you want in an unbelievably better world.

Don't sell the American system short. Before you let anyone attack it, ask him to show you something better.

Don't belittle our competitive society of industry and commerce. It has given us everything we have and it can give us everything we want.

If you will just remember and believe those three short messages, this will be the most successful commencement address ever made.

First, of these three subjects, perhaps it is most difficult for you and me to see the future in the same perspective. You have more of it ahead of you than I, but I have seen more of the past than you.

Your vision today may be sharply honed by the imperfections of our time, but mine is enriched by the knowledge that the world does indeed get better with time. It always has, through history!

We all know that a virus has been spreading across our land and even throughout the world in recent years—the virus of pessimism.

Those afflicted with it see everything as being wrong, and nothing as being right. They call for change and even revolution. They would sweep aside knowledge and order and decency. They would destroy, they say, in order to rebuild. . . .

The next time you hear someone say conditions in the world are bad, ask him just one question: Compared to what? Compared to sixty years ago, when I was born? Compared to the world of a hundred years ago? Compared to the Dark Ages of the past?

More progress already has been made in my lifetime than in all of mankind's history before us, but we have seen only the beginning of the possible. . . .

Never before has so much human fulfillment been possible. On every side of us there is a burgeoning awareness of the humanities and a concern for our fellow human beings.

Incredible worlds of scientific achievement have only begun to be discovered.

And the economic abundance which most of us already have now is coming within the reach of us all.

With remarkable determination and unimaginable speed, this nation is tearing down the walls which once imprisoned men and their opportunities in the ghettos of ignorance and poverty. . . .

In such a country and in such a time, the future is limited only by the horizon each man creates for himself. However quaint it may sound in these days of the twentieth century, opportunity is unlimited. For the young the formula is as plain and simple as it always has been: fix a goal . . . aim high . . . set out to achieve it . . . and you will!

And now a few words about the American system.

In its broadest definition, this system by which we live is woven from three principal strands—political democracy, a free private economy, and universal opportunity.

Those changes which are now taking place in our way of life—those improvements which are now taking place in our nation—are the natural evolutions of this system. . . .

For two centuries this system has assured the United States of growth and greatness, far beyond any country.

But whatever yardstick may be used to measure it against any in the world, it has proved far superior to any other way of life contrived or devised by man at any time in human history.

Ask any critic of our society for a better workable system, and his answer can only be the silence of admission or irresponsible demagoguery. . . .

There is only one significant competing system in the world

today, and it cannot begin to match us. Our standard of living is incredibly higher. Our freedom of thought is infinitely greater. Our spiritual strength is unshackled. We reach to the moon ready to share our discoveries with the world, we are committed to serve and protect the less fortunate, and we live with a personal freedom of movement undreamed of by the rest of mankind. . . .

Imbedded in our national conscience there is a deep desire to right the wrongs—to correct the inequities—to make the whole system work better.

Let us address ourselves to those problems—but in the process let's not destroy the system from which our strength flows. . . .

And now I am at the last item I want to discuss.

One of the keystones of our incredible success as a nation is our competitive free enterprise system. The backbone of that system is the American business community. . . .

Recently a Gallup Poll showed that only 6 percent of today's college students expected to go into business or management. Yet American business today is on the threshold of a new age of growth and service, and in honesty it can reach out to the bright young men and women of our time and invite them to participate. . . .

The great comforts and facilities that surround us today are the products of American enterprise. More important, the highest aspiration of people throughout the world is to achieve the standard of living that we have from the superior productive capability of the competitive American system.

Putting aside all considerations of money, politics, and ideology—reducing our judgment to the simplest common denominator—we can see the evidence of what this system means:

To buy a comparable suit of clothes in Soviet Russia takes 183 hours of work. In France it takes 75 hours; in Great Britian 40 hours; and in the United States only 24 hours of work is needed for the same item.

Or if you prefer to judge by another standard, in the United States one worker on a farm now produces enough to feed 42 people. In France, one worker can feed only approximately 6. The figure is about 5 in Italy, and it is one farm worker for only one other person in China.

These are not boastful figures. They are simple illustrations that

73

what we have works better than what anyone else has. They show that our way delivers more for mankind than that of any other country. . . .

Our need today is not nearly so great for new laws as it is for new people who will see in the world of business a full potential for citizenship and service.

American business today is eager to work with the young people of the nation, and to develop constructive change and progress out of your idealism and intellectualism.

Let me assure you that freedom will be kept alive and meaningful as long as young people like you are willing to seize these opportunities that freedom offers, and to make our competitive system work.

So this is my third point of advice to you: Don't belittle our competitive society of industry and commerce. It has given us everything we have and it can give us everything we want.

Some generations before us had to risk death to achieve freedom for America.

Two generations in my time have had to fight to preserve it—for us as a nation and for each of us as an individual.

Your generation, rich in the security of freedom won, has committed itself to the next goal, the perfection of individual liberty.

You demand universal justice. You plead for equality. You curse the darkness of intolerance and dishonesty. And you seek comfort and peace.

Men have sought these goals throughout history—but never with the advantage you have today. You are strong materially. You are secure in our system of law. You have a workable society.

*Maurice H. Stans*


# The Wisdom of the Heart

□ How true it is that we live in an age so aptly described by A. E. Housman.

> I a stranger and afraid,
> In a world I never made.

74

You young people in the morning of your lives with hearts aglow with faith and hope are leaving the peace and quietude of these hallowed university halls to enter a world in which your future lies beset with the fear and the dread of destructive weapons raining a hurricane of death from the skies above.

You are entering a world with the innocence of youth where men and women are afraid that in this age the value of the human being may be overshadowed by that of the machine, and that they may become economic slaves. But I say to you be not deceived and be not afraid. It is not the thermonuclear weapons which will win the struggle of the future.

It is rather the weapons of the spirit, love, trust in Almighty God, honor among men and faith in the goodness of humanity. That is the doctrine this university of the humanities has tried to teach you. . . .

The achieving of a degree in a university is but the beginning of your education. Your years here have provided a springboard from which to leap into the unknown future. But this degree will have lost much of its value if the deepening years do not bring to you in greater measure the magic of music and poetry, the calm and sustaining comfort of philosophy, the peace of a sunset's afterglow, or the thrill and beauty of the spoken word from pulpit and stage—the shrines of God and men.

On this day therefore I wish from the depths of my heart that all the members of the graduating class of Bishop's University may achieve abundant success in this world. You have been trained for achievement—may it be yours.

And yet even as I speak I am mindful that success is not something that anyone can command. You remember Addison's famous lines:

> 'Tis not in mortals to command success
> But we'll do more, Sempronius, we'll deserve it.

Life is an uncertainty, for no man knows what his destiny may be. Yet a university must give its students something still greater than training for success. It must open up to them the inner paths of wisdom. Therein will lie the inner achievement, whatever the outer achievement may be.

What then is wisdom? What is it to be wise? For wisdom is something more valuable than knowledge, more penetrating even than shrewdness, more many-splendored than the grey thing men call realism.

I am well aware of the need in our present age to develop technical skills and scientific knowledge. But while we must meet this technological challenge of our age, we must not confuse the purposes of our life, for in a free nation it is the very breath of a soul's life.

George Santayana expressed it well when he wrote:

Oh world, thou choosest not the better part,
It is not wisdom to be only wise.
And on the inward vision close the eyes.
But it is wisdom to believe the heart.

One is often impressed in this life by how much is missed by those who have not the wisdom to believe the heart. They may live in a world of wonder and beauty, but never behold it.

William Wordsworth in "Peter Bell," wrote of the blind realist:

A primrose by the river's brim,
A yellow primrose was to him,
And it was nothing more.

And again he writes:

The soft blue sky did never melt
Into his heart: he never felt
The witchery of the soft blue sky.

The greatest error that the realist can make is to suspect the imagination as though it were something that leads us into strange fancies and deceits. In George Bernard Shaw's play *Saint Joan*, there is a passage that bears on this very thought. Joan says, "I hear voices telling me what to do. They come of God." Then she is roughly told by her enemies, "They come from your imagination."

And to this she replies, "Of course, that is how the message of God comes to us. . . ."

I say to you that after a long life's pilgrimage wisdom may never be wholly attained, but yet the very search for it is itself a blessed thing.

Far back in the seventeenth century, the English physician and

76

philosopher, Sir Thomas Browne, one of the wisest of men, was writing these words. "Wisdom is God's most beauteous attribute. No man can attain unto it. Yet Solomon pleased God when he desired it."

So may I say to you today, as your chancellor, as you leave these walls, each for your separate unknown destiny in this troubled world, may the desire for wisdom—the wisdom that believes the heart—be your joy, your refuge, and your hope to the very end.

*From an address by John Bassett*

# Remember

□ When you leave here, don't forget why you came.

*Adlai Stevenson to Princeton University Class*

# Preparation for College

□ If the schools cannot or do not send the colleges properly qualified students, the whole fabric of higher education becomes a bridge built on rotten pilings.

*Dr. Whitney Griswold, President, Yale University*

# Being Eccentric

□ While I am not in favor of maladjustment, I view this cultivation of neutrality, this breeding of mental neuters, this hostility to eccentricity and controversy with grave misgiving. One looks back with dismay at the possibility of a Shakespeare perfectly adjusted to bourgeois life in Stratford, a Wesley contentedly administering a country parish, George Washington going to London to receive a barony from George III, or Abraham Lincoln prospering in Springfield with nary a concern for the preservation of the crumbling Union.

*Adlai Stevenson, commencement address at Smith College*

# Man

□ Man is still the greatest miracle and the greatest problem on this earth. *David Sarnoff*

# Education

□ Except in a very few schools ... the expectation of excellence is considered undemocratic, scholastic competition is downgraded as traumatic, and objective standards are jettisoned as unenlightened.

I see the results of all this in my classes every day. Some years ago, when I was teaching in California, I happened to mention Josef Stalin in a lecture, whereupon a student raised his hand and asked, "Who's that?" "Doug," I said, "You surely must be joking! Do you really mean to tell me that you don't know who Stalin was?" "Well," he answered, "you know, I'm a Canadian. I don't keep up much with United States politics." Despite my efforts, he received his degree. . . .

You'd be amazed at some of the remarkable things I learn when grading examination papers. For instance, that "the three divisions within modern Judaism are the Sadducees, the Pharisees, and the Hebrews." That "Jefferson Davis wrote in the Declaration of Independence that 'all men are created equal.' " That "Plato incorporated the views of Aristotle into the philosophy of the Church." . . . That "the object of law is to enforce liberty, equality, and fertility," and that "fertility can be readily enforced." These are statements by college students, some of them seniors. And yet we're told that this generation of college students is the most knowledgeable and articulate that we have ever had.

*Dr. Robert V. Andelson*

# How Many Students?

□ We should not penalize ourselves with concepts of unattainable excellence believing that if every student is not an Edison we have

78

failed. We should be content with the kinds of modest success which characterize other forms of education and training. How many splendid researchers do we turn out each year? How many skilled experimentalists? I don't mean to be cynical but there is some truth in the reply of the college president who when asked, "How many students do you have on your campus?" replied, "About half!"                                                   *Myron Tribus*

# Rights and Responsibilities

□ Congratulations to all you graduates! You look great and I know you are happy. And to you relatives and friends—I share your pride and enthusiasm for their accomplishments. . . . I congratulate you particularly because you made a choice about your future—a choice to continue your education. I believe you will be glad you have made that decision since this accomplishment is something no one can take from you. That gives you a right to be happy.

You know, we hear a great deal about rights today. Right to assemble, picket, complain, march, or destroy. A right to an education, a job, a guaranteed wage, a nice house, a voice in government, a right to "do your own thing." But I for one have heard quite enough dialogue about rights for a while. I'm ready to look at the other side of the coin. I want to talk for a while not about rights, but about responsibility; not about praise, but about challenge; not about guaranteed success, but about opportunity; and not about destruction, but about construction and support.

*Jack L. Davidson*

# The Hope of the Future

□ A good part of the difficulty is that we try to educate everybody, and wind up educating practically nobody. We have a mania for quantity. We seem to think that the more colleges we build and the more students we dragoon into them, the more educated our population will become. This is a fallacy. There are altogether too many people in college now who have no business being there—people who didn't come to cultivate their minds, but came to please their parents, or to snag a husband, or to avoid the draft. And, since all too often the level of instruction is geared to them, many of them manage to survive and get their sheepskins without ever having really known what it is to engage in intellectual activity. So we are surfeited with third-rate professionals: teachers who are barely literate, business executives who are weak in economics, engineers who have trouble with a slide rule, radio announcers who mispronounce the simplest English words. And while droves of ill-prepared and poorly motivated people are sporting baccalaureate and even graduate degrees, it's next to impossible to find a competent mechanic or chef or electrician.

To those of you who are being graduated from Union Academy this evening, let me say this. Don't let anybody push you into college against your will. If you aren't sincerely interested in obtaining a liberal education, and if you aren't prepared to pay the price in rigorous application that such an education requires, don't become part of the problem. Don't make my job that much harder. There is a desperate demand all over this country today for honest craftsmen—for people who know how to work effectively with their hands, and who take pride in manual accomplishments. Consider that to be a good plumber is infinitely more honorable than to be a slipshod scientist or an incompetent attorney—and, these days, it's likely to be more lucrative, too!

But if you have a thirst for humane knowledge; if you have learned here how to stretch your minds, and want to keep on stretching them—come to us. We need you and we want you. And when you come, be persevering. Remember that amid all the spoonfeeding and busy-working and rat-capping and hellraising, amid the Cliff notes and the roll calls and the snap tests and the beer busts—amid and in spite of all these things, if you seek diligently enough, and study hard enough, and wait long enough, you may find a couple of professors who will inspire you, and four or five books which will open new vistas for you. And, as these professors and these books force you to think, who knows? Who knows but what out of your thinking may arise constructive ways of dealing with the terrible and solemn issues which imperiously confront our nation and our world?

In this lies the hope of the future, perhaps the only hope. "Not in wild dreams of red destruction nor weak projects for putting men in leading strings to a brainless abstraction called the State," but in this. For, as a great American sage and prophet, Henry George, wrote many years ago:

> Social reform is not to be secured by noise and shouting; by complaints and denuniciations; by the formation of parties; or the making of revolutions; but by the awakening of thought and the progress of ideas. Until there be correct thought, there can be no right action; and when there is correct thought, right action will follow. *Dr. Robert V. Andelson*

# Thinking

□ People have got to think. Thinking isn't to agree or disagree. That's voting. *Robert Frost*

# Picking a College

□ Helping your eldest son pick a college is one of the next educational experiences of life—for the parents. Next to trying to pick his bride, it's the best way to learn that your authority, if not entirely gone, is slipping fast. *Sally and James Reston,*
*Saturday Evening Post*

# An Honor

□ No greater nor more affectionate honor can be conferred on an American than to have a public school named after him.
*Herbert Hoover*

# The Other Side of the Coin

□ A society full of doubts, a society in turmoil, a society reflecting anxiety, is a society which often is destructive. Such a society can be destructive of physical things as well as being destructive of thoughts, emotions, feelings, and character. Certain elements of our society today tend to be destructive. People find themselves dissatisfied with events which affect their lives. . . . As a result of these feelings they tend to become destructive with their own attitudes so that their general philosophy is one of sweeping criticism and all-inclusive condemnation. Everything is bad; nothing is good. It is an open trap into which many of our citizens are falling. But, it is an easy way out of our troubled times. I submit to you that the other side of that coin is construction and support, rather than destruction and condemnation. It is legitimate inquiry and protest to object to certain actions but it is responsible citizenship to carry with that objection a suggested solution to the problem. It is one thing to disagree with public officials; it is another thing to refuse them the right and the opportunity to express their views. It is one thing to see a need for change and reform; it is something quite different to attempt to enforce that reform with force and gunpowder. There is much in our society today for which to be thankful. Much is being accomplished on all fronts; granted much remains to be done, but our nation as well as our community can only deteriorate to the point where its citizens will allow it to deteriorate. Constructive respect for our country and its heritage can only be destroyed if we are willing to allow it to be destroyed. The family as an entity can be dissolved only if we are willing to allow it to be dissolved. Destruction of many of the basic tenets of our society is one side of the coin and we hear about this a great deal today, but constructive support is the other side of the coin about which we need to hear a great deal more. Support and encouragement go a long way down the road toward improvement. Improvement and change make for all of us a better life.

I hope you will have occasion to reflect on the need to look at the other side of the coin. To recall that with each right comes an accompanying responsibility; that praise has its place but that challenge is even more important; that we need not guarantee success even though we must guarantee opportunity; and that destruction accomplishes nothing for our society, but constructive support can accomplish great things. I wish for you continued success and a desire to examine "the other side of the coin."

*Jack L. Davidson*

# True Leadership

□ America has need of thousands of leaders who will never be elected president or even a governor of a state or president of a professional society, but who, quietly and without ostentation, nevertheless will exert true leadership in their several walks of life.

*Dr. Harold W. Dodds,*
*baccalaureate address at Princeton University*

# Help of the Young

□ A society which allows its young to be spiritually cut adrift is a society which cuts itself off from its own future. The complex and difficult tasks of today and tomorrow demand patience and persistence and unity of effort, and of none is this more true than the slow labor of building a more secure peace stone by careful stone. We need the understanding and help of the young, as you need ours. The work, in any case, cannot long continue without your help, for it will soon be yours to do if it is to be done at all. In "The People, Yes," Carl Sandburg wrote,

> Man is a long time coming.
> Man will yet win.
> Brother may yet line up with brother.

I can only add, "Amen."

*From a commencement ceremony*
*by Elliot L. Richardson*
*at Lowell Technological Institute*

# The Same Appeal

□ Year after year these congregations [at Yale University baccalaureate] hear the same exhortations, the same appeals to youth to sally forth, knight-errant, and slay the same old dragons in the same old sinful world. Yet these dragons, unlike their mortal cousins the dinosaurs, have managed to keep well ahead of the game. If Darwin himself had picked them as favorites in the cosmic sweepstakes, they could not have run a better race.

*Whitney Griswold*

# The Essence of Education

□ Many of the alienated young protest that a diploma represents sixteen years of conditioning by society, learning to jump meaningless hurdles at the command of the Establishment. For them, the three R's mean "Rules, Respect, and Rote." But we have enough examples of men who were set free—introduced to great ideas, given a deeper understanding of people, and rigorous training in logical thought—to discount this argument. A second view holds that education is what education does—lectures in class, study of notes and books, exams, and extracurriculars such as good, oldfashioned hell-raising, social and athletic events, and commencements. These activities have their value—a solid factual background, self-discipline, the ability to get along among people— but they are only forms which have been grafted onto the skeleton of education.

The essence of education, and its value, are not in such external forms, but are internal, part of the educated man himself. Education means exposure to ideas; it is the ability to live and work with people very different from us; it is the ability to draw something meaningful from daily life. . . .

Finally, the educated man is tolerant. Nothing has torn America more these last few years than intolerance—students who shout down speakers or throw pies in their faces rather than listen to them; hardhats who maul peaceful demonstrators; anyone who uses force to prevent another from peaceably stating his views is doing his part to destroy America. People often say that, in a showdown, the orthodoxy of the right will prevail over the absolutism of the left—but this misses the point; no such orthodoxy, no such absolutism should be upheld in the first place. . . .

Tolerance is the midwife of peaceful change—intolerance will lead only to repression on the one hand and revolutionism on the other. Either way, the results are the same: broken bodies in the

84

streets, and flaming hatred in men's hearts. Our society can do better than these grisly alternatives; men who are tolerant insure that it will.

I have selected examples from the political right and left, from young and old, from the formally educated and those with less schooling, because I believe that education is more than a matter of classroom learning. Rather, it is an outlook on life. Clearly, it doesn't take a college degree to practice the qualities I've mentioned. There are as many men without diplomas who deserve the title, "educated," as there are men with degrees who do not. The diplomas we receive do not say, "you are educated." They only say that we're in a good position to try.

And so today is not so much a celebration of accomplishment as it is a service of dedication for all of us, parents and friends as well as graduates, to commit our minds, our talents, our lives to the best qualities that education offers.

For more than two weeks last month, the flag behind you flew at half-staff—mute testimony to our need for all the honest, committed, reasonable and tolerant citizens we can produce. If we fail, our loss will be all mankind's. If we succeed, we shall have an age of peace and love among men—a true Age of Aquarius.

*Excerpts from a commencement address*
*at Wabash College by Richard White*

# Self-Knowledge

□ . . . At the height of our power we hesitate because we can see in a terrifying self-knowledge the necessity of putting reason before will, persuasion before assertiveness, asking before answering, concern before self-regard. . . . *Nathan Pusey*

# Our Accomplishments

□ The thing which really disappoints me is the lack of understanding and appreciation for the American dream. America is composed of sinful human beings, America has her faults and shortcomings, but they pale into insignificance alongside the accomplishments and fulfillment of the American Way. There is a theme in our national heritage which can cause us to walk together to the music of distant drums. Bancroft, the general historian, commenting on the Mayflower Compact signed on that tiny boat off the Massachusetts coast, said that in the opening words, "In the Name of God, Amen," was the birthplace of constitutional liberty. . . .

We have faced difficult times in American history before. When Washington was at Valley Forge, the future of our country seemed to be in total jeopardy. A third of Washington's men had deserted, a third died from malnutrition and only a scant third were left who were able-bodied. Yet in the snows of that incredible winter, prayers were answered and out of the travail came the victory of the American Revolution. What could have been more hopeless than Lincoln during the Civil War when brother was fighting brother and hate and distrust engulfed the country? Time after time Lincoln and his cabinet turned to God and, believing that they had found His purpose for this country, they endured and the nation was saved.                    *Dr. Robert J. Lamont*


# What Is Man?

□ There is no mathematical formula by which you can settle the problem of what you will be and what you will stand for. As the Princetonian editor expressed it, it is a problem which everyone must solve for himself. How you decide relates to your sensitivity to human values, to your allegiance to those unique qualities of the spirit which mark mankind off from even the highest animals.

In conclusion, may I relate what I have been saying to the nature of these baccalaureate exercises, which traditionally take the form of a religious service in our chapel, dedicated to the abiding truths of our faith. It is our belief that God is daily manifesting Himself in us, His creatures and His children, that validates our worth and glory as individuals with a peculiar destiny of our own. It is our personal relationship to a supernatural being which sets "an absolute value on the dignity of every human being." Saint Paul tells us not to be conformed to this world but to be transformed that we "may prove what is the good and acceptable and perfect will of God." As our faith supports the integrity and autonomy of the individual, so does it impose the grave but noble obligation to be one. That divine thirst for some purpose and permanence to our existence as autonomous individuals, the universal search to which the Roman emperor Hadrian referred, summons us to obedience to a Personal Being outside ourselves and yet an integral part of us as individuals; and in response to this summons we find fulfillment.

There are a good many influences these days, more than I have time to mention, which can readily lead a man to assume that the courage which it takes to face the loneliness and unease of being oneself represents but a futile gesture against overwhelming forces.

Now that astronomy has shown us that man is physically less than a speck in an immeasurable universe; now that our big society is modifying the social relations of the individual to others, now that we know more about the influence of social trends on conduct, more about the play of unconscious psychological incentives and more about the chemistry of the brain, man's erstwhile purely rational view of himself has suffered some sharp shocks. But the self-conscious human being has survived, and, I promise you, will continue to survive. The more science can tell us about the natural aspects of our world and of ourselves, the more will our human and spiritual energies be released to express themselves. Science and technology do not diminish personality, unless we want it that way.

In moving poetic language the composer of the eighth Psalm summarizes all and more than I have said this morning. First he refers to the question which I have just mentioned and which no thoughtful person can escape: Is not the individual man too minute a particle in vast space, or as we might say in this modern age of social mechanism, to be of any significance in himself? The psalmist puts the question to the Lord in this way:

> When I consider thy heavens, the work of thy fingers,
> The moon and the stars, which thou hast ordained,
> What is man, that thou art mindful of him?
> And the son of man, that thou visitest him?

It is, I repeat, a natural question for us moderns, as it was for the psalmist. But he wavers only for a moment; promptly he goes on

87

to reassure us regarding man's sovereign place in all creation in the memorable sentences:

> For thou hast made him a little lower than the angels,
> And hast crowned him with glory and honor.
> Thou madest him to have dominion over the works of thy hands;
> Thou hast put all things under his feet.

If you remember this through all the years to come you will not be seduced into depersonalizing conformity; you will be an individual. I commend it, not as a man learned in theology or the doctrines of the Church, but as an ordinary citizen who has found that this faith is both rational and practical. It is a mystery, I know, but so in the deepest sense is tomorrow's sunrise or the prospect that you will be graduated on Tuesday.

*Harold W. Dodds, then President of Princeton University*

# Inner Simplicity

□ It was not the outer grandeur of the Roman but the inner simplicity of the Christian that lived on through the ages.

*Charles Lindbergh*

# Men's Heads

□ They had men's heads on men's shoulders.　　　*Frank Bailey*

# A Student

□ A student is not a professional athlete. . . . He is not a little politician or junior senator looking for angles . . . an amateur promoter, a gladhander, embryo Rotarian, café-society leader, quiz kid, or man about town. A student is a person who is learning to fulfill his powers and to find ways of using them in the service of mankind.　　　*Dr. Harold Taylor*

# Prayer—By a High School Senior

☐ When we look back and see all the way You have brought us, we are joyful and have a thankful heart. But we want more people to share our joy in a new and a better world. We pray for this our troubled world, our perplexed world, walking in the vague light of an uncertain peace. In our hearts, we know that ours is not a true peace but rather one of blatant suspicion and fear, animosity and greed. Lord, we ask that Your Spirit will guide the leaders of the world as they seek a way in which all the peoples of the world can live at peace with one another and with themselves.

Lord, impress upon the hearts and the minds of the world's leaders and upon our minds and hearts that we must first be at peace with You before we can be at peace with anyone else—that freedom must exist everywhere if it is to exist anywhere, that the strength of a nation does not lie in armies or navies, but in the integrity of its people, that peace can only be born out of righteousness, that the trouble with our world is only people—and nothing else, that the direction of men's minds, wills, and hearts and our minds and hearts must be changed if peace is to exist.

Make us willing to be changed, whatever the cost to our self-sufficiency or insistence on having our own way.

Lord, please reveal Your will for our country that we may now see our destiny and place in Your plans for the future and the world.

Dear Lord, Our Father, grant that the day may come fast when culture and learning, empathy and pity, shall light all the lamps that wars have extinguished; when all men shall be brothers the world over despite differences in color, creed, or nationality; when all of us will be united in the task of building a new and a better world. In Your name. the Father of us all, we make this prayer. Amen.

*Carl Smiley of Winchester, Massachusetts.*
*From* Praying Hands

# Have Faith

☐ Have faith in yourself. Don't underestimate yourself. The greatest waste on earth is the waste of human potential—the waste of what men and women could be if they only had enough faith in themselves to develop their talents and abilities.

Have faith in your fellowman. I know life is competitive—but it isn't a jungle. Like begets like. Faith inspires faith. People give back substantially what we give to them.

And then—have faith in America. Don't sell your country short.

America isn't perfect. We ought to be impatient with its imperfections. We have plenty of reason for constructive discontent and plenty of room for improvement. But do not be misled. America is not just another nation. It is not only rich and powerful. It is the trustee of mankind's hope for freedom and human fulfillment.

You and I are fortunate to be Americans. Because of the vision of the founders and builders of America, we have the opportunity to develop ourselves, shape our destinies, and build a greater nation and a better world. America's revolutionary principles of freedom, equality, and opportunity are universal. They are meant not only for Americans, but for all the people of the world—that all men everywhere may free themselves from every form of bondage and have an equal chance in life.

That is the destiny and purpose of America. And that is a vision worthy of your faith.

*Excerpts from a commencement address*
*at Bethany College, West Virginia*

# Freedom

□ Humility says to us, "You must always keep in the back of your mind the idea, maybe only a tiny idea, that perhaps you may be wrong." In the words of Oliver Cromwell when he once spoke to an enemy, "By the bowels of Christ, I beseech you, bethink you that you may be mistaken." And it is that element, the idea that all of us know we could be mistaken, even though of course we know we are not, which is the fundamental reason we must support and foster the freedom to speak, the freedom to listen, the freedom to compete, and freedoms in as many spheres of our lives as possible.

Fundamentally, there are only two ways in which men can live together. They can either do so voluntarily or they can do so through compulsion. Freedom is the only alternative to coercion.

*From an address by Dr. Milton Friedman*
*at a Rockford College commencement*

# Men of Honor

◻ It seems to me that it might be well for us to recall this morning that there are men of honor and integrity as well as the sort about whom we read daily. I am indebted to William Hazlitt, English essayist, for the idea. "There is a time to praise famous men and our fathers that begat us. The Lord manifested in them great glory, even His mighty power from the beginning." It seemed fitting for us to do this on this Sunday which falls between the birth dates of our two greatest Americans: Washington and Lincoln. In thinking of the great and good, we need always to remember our obligation and theirs to the unknown and faithful. Somewhere during that awful winter of Valley Forge there was a young man with bleeding feet who remained at his post. Without him and his fellows the story of Washington would be different. Somewhere in that awful hour at Gettysburg on Cemetery Hill a boy stood and did not run and perhaps died. Because he stood, his squad stood; because his squad stood, his company stood; because his company stood, others stood and the battle was won, and the tide of war turned. We have an eternal obligation to the unknown heroes of war and peace. Other men stood on their shoulders and are held faithful by them. God knows their names and He who notes the sparrow's fall will remember. There is a greatness known only to God. *Dr. Harrison Ray Anderson*

# A Prayer of Thanks

◻ Eternal God and Father of us all, we pause before Thee to offer our thanks for the privilege of citizenship in a nation of free men;

for the right to choose those who shall lead us in the years to come; for men of integrity and courage who are willing to assume the mantles of leadership, and for the undiscourageable hope that both peace and justice may bless the days to come. Keep us aware, we pray, that we dwell under the sovereignty of Thy great spirit.

We are grateful, Gracious Lord, for the beauty and the bounty of our beloved land. Grant that we may preserve it for the generations coming on. We thank Thee for those who speak the truth with conviction and integrity and for men and women whose spirit honors the arena of political life. Bless us this night and accept our gratitude for Thy blessings and fellowship, and for the high responsibilities that challenge us. We pray in the Master's name. Amen.                                 *Dr. Harold Blake Walker*

# Go Forth and Be Strong

□ What then can I say to you at the end of your college years? It must be, I think, that neither unreasoning zealotry nor despair is an acceptable attitude for Harvard men. You have seen much of one and, I suspect, have at least occasionally been tempted by the other. It has been said that your generation is the first in America to have grown up without optimism. This is a sad commentary if true. Personally I do not believe that it is, or at least that it need be.

It has been remarked by many, however, that you have a widespread and deep feeling of helplessness because you see so many things that need to be set right and feel so powerless to effect change. If so, such feeling is not without justification. But you must not assume you are the first to have felt this way, for it is a feeling with which the concerned have always had to contend.

In such mood it is easy to denounce, to find fault, to make unjust accusations, to visit the shortcomings of the world, and of ourselves, on scapegoats—even to light fires or throw stones—for personal relief or for exploitation—easy and totally unworthy. It is more difficult to maintain a realistic sense of human limitation, to refuse to become frustrated and angry; to analyze, to assess, to seek to understand and explain; to determine to be adult and fair;

and thus to work patiently to improve while refusing to succumb to either cynicism or hopelessness. It is a long way around, but it is the civilized way, and the only way for those who have come truly to understand the role of humane learning.

It is this kind of behavior which Harvard has always wanted to teach—or rather has hoped that it might in some degree exemplify in its teachers and teachings, and so strongly represent that those coming here to learn would inevitably find it for themselves—and finding it, be beguiled by its charm and sign on for life in allegiance to it.

I may put it this way: there is a world of reason, modesty, charity, and trust in the midst of, and opposed to, the oppressive and contentious world of deceit, anger, vilification, and self-righteousness now made so manifest all about us . . . by would-be exploiters. This former world is created and precariously maintained in all generations by civilized men, a world for which in the depths of our hearts I am sure we all yearn. What I have wanted to say to you today is simply that in my view, as Harvard men, you are called to serve that world.

In earlier days at this baccalaureate service Harvard presidents have tried first to suggest this world and have then reiterated again a requirement to work for it, a basic tenet in our enduring liberal tradition. Life outside the academy was probably no more easy then than now, nor did my predecessors have any illusions about the difficulty and the only limited chances of what they were asking. But finally in a deep intent to be helpful they would go on to say, quite unashamedly, "Go forth and be strong."

Styles change, circumstances change. But from what we have been through here together in your years and from what we have now come to sense of the difficulties and the dangers of this time, it seems to me we have earned the right again to speak in such terms.

In a world of violence, deceit and coercive evil—to experience which, most regrettably, you have not had to wait to go outside—wishing in my turn to be helpful I would first pray for you clarity of vision. Then in a period as troubled and uncertain as any in our history, echoing my predecessors' words, I would say something quite similar to what has been said here so many times in the past, urging you not, from a feeling of helplessness, either to surrender to rage or to succumb to self-pity, but rather to go forth and be strong. Beyond this, since in such enterprise you will surely need help—as others who have gone before you have needed help—I would add a further prayer, that the grace of God may go with you and sustain you wherever you go and in whatever task to which you will be called.

Yours has been a college generation full of difficulty, doubt, and confusion. Yet I would be lacking a fundamental faith in the wonder-working of this university if I were not convinced you will find, in retrospect, your time in college to have been extraordinarily maturing and rewarding. Difficulty brings self-knowledge. Out of trouble springs inner strength and self-renewal. We see now in part only through the darkened glass. It will be your task to help make that vision clearer for yourself and for those near and dear to you through courage, faith, hope, and love which have sustained others before you through trials every bit as great as yours. Go forth and be strong.          *Nathan L. Pusey*

# Abuse of the Great

□ The abuse that men in public, in church, and state have to take is tragic. Recently I have read again of the attacks on Washington when he was a general. He could not reply to his critics without endangering his troops and the American cause. Finally, however, he sat down on a cold night, December 23, 1777, and wrote, "I can assure these gentlemen that it is a much easier and less distressing thing to draw remonstrances in a comfortable room by a good fireside than to occupy a cold, bleak hill and sleep under frost and snow, without clothes and blankets. However, although they seem to have little feeling for the naked and distressed soldiers, I feel superabundantly for them, and from my soul, I pity those miseries which it is neither in my power to relieve or prevent." A soldier to his critics! Washington—"first in war—first in peace, and" for a long time—"first in the hearts of his countrymen." No longer is this true, for Lincoln has that place! Gaunt and good; Old Testament prophet of righteous justice, he felt and spoke through a Christian heart of compassion and sorrow.

What friends Lincoln and Lee would have been. Lee hated slavery for what it did to his fellow whites of the South. Lincoln hated it for what it did to the nation as a whole. "I believe," wrote Lee, "I believe a kind God has ordered all things for our good." So Lee could accept defeat and turn it into victory.

*Dr. Harrison Ray Anderson*

# I Shall Do

◻ I believe anyone whom you encourage and help to think and rethink in today's crisis will find his thought leading him back to things that are basic in American life—freedom, sanctity of the home, thrift, work, each man and each woman making his small contribution to the whole by trying, by what we used to call "right living."

Let us make the point that other generations of Americans have had their crises, too—their bloody wars, their long-lasting and soul-searching depressions, their riots, and even their threats of imminent extinction—and yet America has indeed made remarkable progress, largely by adhering to principles which may seem old-fashioned.

To sum up, the resolution of today's crisis in American life must begin with each individual. The relationship which you and I have with members of our immediate families is the beginning of a chain reaction. Within our family groups, we must teach and learn understanding, reasonableness, justice, love, fidelity, patriotism, love of God—for then and only then will we achieve the love of our fellowman which, I believe, can and will save the country and the world.

Edward Hale, a former chaplain of the United States Senate, sums it all up nicely for us in these words:

"I am only one, but I am one. I can't do everything, but I can do something. And what I can do, that I ought to do, and what I ought to do, by the grace of God, I shall do."

*From a commencement address*
*by Frank Blair, Newscaster*
*for the National Broadcasting Company*

# Achievements

▫ Let's assume that in 1869 we were given five projects to be completed one hundred years later:

1) Design a highway system to handle the traffic one hundred years from then.

2) Design a method for efficiently delivering the mail.

3) Design a box which when you turn a knob you can see things happening in color in other parts of the country.

4) Design a device which will communicate voices around the world.

5) Design a device which will transport three hundred people coast to coast within four hours.

In 1869 we would probably choose project one and two as those we could successfully accomplish within one hundred years—the other three as "impossible" to accomplish.

Yet look what has actually happened. The three "impossible" tasks we have accomplished through private enterprise, while the two "possible" tasks which have been tackled by government are still to be accomplished.

*James R. Evans*


# A Lifelong Concern

▫ My personal congratulations to members of the first graduating class of 1969 of Northern Michigan University. The sacrifice that you and your relatives have made to achieve the education this ceremony commemorates is substantial in quantity and symbolic in quality. It is substantial in human energy as well as in money. It symbolizes the determination of man to contribute to the world as much as his very great abilities allow.

Having made this sacrifice and having attained a recognized high level of achievement, you have a deep and sacred obligation to continue to be devoted to your fellowman. If you accept this obligation, almost certainly you will find that your concern with universities is continual. Rather than leaving higher education at this point in your life, your participation in higher education will be just beginning. Education is a lifelong concern of every thoughtful citizen wishing to improve the lot of man. You will be increasingly concerned with the manner in which higher education relates to the many facets of the broader society.

*Edward W. Weidner, Chancellor,*
*University of Wisconsin, Green Bay*

# Two Considerations

□ Two considerations should, in my opinion, guide our thoughts. The first is a sense of the magnitude as well as the preciousness of time. I ask you to reflect on the period of written history alone, a period which represents only a fraction of the span of human life on this planet, and a minute fraction of the span of life itself. Visualize, if you will, these approximately five thousand years, described by the face of a clock. If today were represented by high noon, it would not be until 11:15 A.M. with some forty-five minutes to go until today, that the clock would mark the arrival of Pere Marquette and Louis Joliet to this region. The founding of Lind University, the precursor to this college, would be marked only when the hands were at 11:44. A long time back in years, but a short time on the clock!

Perhaps even more surprising, the crucial last twenty-five years would be ticked off in only the last four minutes on the clock. These are the years between the bomb at Hiroshima and the contemporary terror of the Jordanian desert, the years when problems of urbanization, pollution, race relations, war, and lack of leadership have threatened the ability of mankind to live together as equals, with a sense of dignity and respect for others; indeed, threatened the ability of mankind to continue to live at all. These are the years . . . when the American college has been besieged by numbers, endowed with unprecedented wealth, respected and supported by government, but still found wanting in purpose, direction, or, sadly, commitment. These are the years when the undergraduate has too often been forgotten for the sake of the graduate, and teaching too often forgotten for the benefit of research.

Will the next five or ten years abolish forever the treasures and the truths of civilization, either by relegating them to the musty stacks of unused libraries or burying them in the ashes of our technological advance? It is the task of institutions of higher learning, and particularly the liberal arts college, to assure that this not be the case, and that civilization continues to respect the past as it serves as guardian for the present. Time is both a precious and a scarce commodity.

The second consideration which I urge you to bear in mind is not unrelated to the first. Lake Forest College was founded and has developed as a liberal arts college supported by private funds. This fact both gives us our special opportunity and restricts our course.

I am not here tonight to defend a liberal arts education, although I could do so passionately and with conviction. I assume that all of you share this conviction or you would not be here yourselves today. In some ways, our task is more difficult than that of a university where research can be king and vocational and professional training his consorts. In a university, the measure is apt to be quantitative and objective; in a college it must be qualitative and subjective. Our work is defined by the free search for truth by students and by teachers and the free exchange of ideas without fear or control; our tablet must include all of written history, as well as our hopes and dreams for the future; our challenge is to relate with meaning the problems of today with the wisdom of the past. It is up to the liberal arts college to discover the relationship between our vast technological skills which carry with them the potential of the destruction of all of mankind and the limits of freedom which must be imposed if mankind is to survive. It is up to the liberal arts college to develop within its students the leadership capabilities necessary to guide others in the exercise of these skills and this freedom.

A liberal arts education is not everyone's bag! But particularly as a private college, we must avoid the obvious danger of basing our selection on social elitism, but rather seek to admit students because of their stated commitment to the goals of a liberal arts education. We must also exploit the potential for innovation so peculiarly ours because of our private rather than public support, and give to those who want to pursue truth an opportunity to find excitement and, indeed, "relevance" in their college experience. If we accomplish this, we have succeeded where most have tried and failed. Because we acted from purpose and not default, we shall also have nurtured the promise while subduing the danger which confronts us today.

Dr. Eugene Hotchkiss III, President, Lake Forest College

# What One Learns from the Library

□ Rush Rhees Library, on the George Eastman Quadrangle at the University of Rochester, bears on either side of its main portals two inscriptions from which generations of students have drawn inspiration. The inscription to the left of the library doors reads:

Here is the history of human ignorance, error, superstition, folly, war, and waste, recorded by human intelligence for the admonition of wiser ages still to come.

The other inscription reads:

Here is the history of man's hunger for truth, goodness, and beauty, leading him slowly on through flesh to spirit, from bondage to freedom, from war to peace.

Inside that library, as inside thousands of libraries all over America, much can be learned about ignorance, error, superstition, folly, war, and waste; and much can be learned about truth, goodness, beauty, the human spirit, freedom, and peace.

There are, to be sure, important things that cannot be learned in libraries, or elsewhere in universities. Some of them can be learned only on battlefields, in hospitals, in slums, in artists' studios, in factories, banks, and stores, or from the experience of life itself; and some important truths cannot be grasped at all in youth. But in our libraries and elsewhere in our colleges and universities much knowledge and wisdom can be acquired that is not likely to be acquired elsewhere.

War, poverty, injustice, and limitations of freedom are enormously complex problems. Yet the history of the past decade, the

99

past generation, the past century, and longer shows that progress has occurred on all of these problems—not uninterrupted progress, perhaps; not sufficient progress, surely; but enough progress over long enough periods to demonstrate that it can happen.

*W. Allen Wallis*

# Opening Prayer at the Annual Mayor's Prayer Breakfast in Chicago

□ O God allow me to salute You in the name of all here present. We are just a few of Your children, but we feel we do represent the millions who fill our city. Every heart therefore is influenced by this dedication and through the unity of purpose we believe many of our men and women will profit from Your most gracious acceptance.

It would indeed be wrong for any selfishness to stain this morning's efforts. No cause could be of greater moment than for us to recognize Your mastery over us and to demonstrate our willingness to serve. We acknowledge Your sovereignty, we readily admit our dependence.

We come before You in prayerful contemplation, realizing that all the wonderful things of nature that surround us have been entrusted to the care of Your creatures and that their proper use can bring happiness to mankind; while on the other hand, their abuse can cause unnecessary sorrow and grief. Perhaps nowhere on earth is there such abundance as we find in our own land. America, the state of Illinois, the city of Chicago have been singularly blessed. We are indeed some of the most fortunate ones because we have been able to enjoy these benefits that are within such easy reach.

For all of this we are grateful; first of all, to You, the Almighty Father who has inspired us with the fundamental truths; and secondly to all of our officials, executives, men and women of the various professions, the teachers in our schools, in our churches and synagogues who have established a leadership in fashioning a program of direction toward right living.

We thank You, especially for the breath of life whereby we become Your creatures, and for the intellect whereby we reason out our existence, and for the infusion of Your divine help to give us an insight into our destiny. Without these supernatural infused virtues we would not produce the divine-human acts which lead to the vision of God.

The world of the supernatural is familiar to God. It is His own world. But it is not familiar to man. If man is to make his way safely and easily in this world, he must be led by God. Human reason is a sufficient guide to man in the natural world. But in the world of God human reason is not an accurate guide. Human reason may enable man to live in peace and contentment with other men. But God is infinite perfection. Therefore man must seek God's help to make sound and lasting progress in a society troubled by fear and hate. God has provided this help through the gifts and fruits of the Holy Spirit—wisdom, counsel, fear of the Lord, charity, joy, peace, patience.

We find ourselves gathered together this morning but we are all so different. In the eyes of man's world we might walk separate paths. In the eyes of God there is only one path. God, this very day, is looking into hearts and souls. We can only fulfill our destiny by drinking from the same cup—God's cup which contains His love for all of His children.

We pray to be refreshed this morning by His heavenly blessings and to go forth with brotherly love to bring joy and peace to our fellowmen. May we not be discomforted by unnecessary strife and senseless animosity for as children of the Heavenly Father we believe in One God, One Aim and One Destiny.

May peace abide with us. Amen.

*John H. Sengstacke, Publisher,*
*Chicago Daily Defender* and *Pittsburgh Courier*

# Freedom to Speak and Freedom to Listen

□ Freedom to speak means freedom to try to persuade other people to listen to you if you have something to say, or to try to make them think you have something to say. It does not stand by itself. It is part of a much broader tradition. As an economist, I naturally think in terms of its economic analog. I think it helps us understand the role of freedom of speech if we think of its

76711

counterpart in economics. The counterpart of freedom of speech in economics is the freedom to compete, the freedom to produce something and to try to persuade somebody to buy it. The freedom to compete does not mean the right to have customers. It does not mean that anybody who wants to is entitled to make you buy from them. Indeed the two are completely inconsistent. Compulsory customers is the opposite of freedom of competition, of freedom to produce.

There is no difference in the marketplace of ideas. Freedom of speech is simply freedom of competition in the world of ideas, in the world of thought. It is the right to offer your wares in the marketplace of ideas, and to try to attract customers to it. It is not the right to hit anybody over the head to make them be your customers. Freedom to compete in the marketplace for goods does not mean that I have the right to enter your house, to put my wares before you. If I am an energetic salesman, I may knock at your door and try to get you to listen to me. I may ask you whether you will invite me in and see what it is I have to sell. But no one would argue that my freedom to sell, my freedom to compete, includes my freedom to break down your door and to say to you, "You listen to me or else."

This is equally true in the marketplace of ideas. I have the right to offer my ideas to whoever wants to listen. I have no right to enter a person's house and force him to listen to my ideas. I have no right to stop a car on the highway and say "You must listen to me." I have no right to take over a building and say that building shall be occupied by me until you listen to me. And typically—to bring in another current confusion—those who occupy the building mean not "until you listen to me," but "until you are persuaded." The freedom to listen means the freedom to reject what you are told as well as to accept what you are told, just as economic freedom means the freedom to buy or to refuse to buy.

Freedom of speech means that I have a right to hire a hall and see if I can persuade anybody to come. The right to hire a hall, the right to put yourself up for people to listen to you is no mean right. If you consider the episodes that have been going on in the Soviet Union over the past several years, you will see that this is no mean right. Let the small number of courageous protesters in the Soviet Union try to hire a hall. They will not find one for rent. Their constitution guarantees freedom of speech in words but it is an empty guarantee when it is not accompanied by the dispersion of power which permits a person to hire a hall in which to talk and which protects him from losing his job if he says something that is not attractive to the people in power. Ask Sinayevsky and Daniel, and their more recent brave compatriots, as they languish in jail for taking the Soviet Constitution at its word. Protection of the freedom to speak and the freedom to listen is provided by the dispersion of power which comes from the wide ownership of property, from the fact that there are many people from whom you can hire a hall. All these freedoms are a bundle. The freedom to listen is as absent in totalitarian countries as the freedom to speak.

*From an address by Dr. Milton Friedman*
*at a Rockford College commencement*

# A Nation Under God

□ In these days when religion is not supposed to be fashionable in many quarters, when skepticism and even agnosticism seem to be on the upturn, over half of all the letters that have come to our office have indicated that people of all faiths and of all backgrounds, in a very simple way are saying, "We are praying for you, Mr. President. We are praying for this country. We are praying for the leadership."

Two days ago I spent four hours with one of the theoreticians of the "New Left." We debated, we fought, we disagreed, we agreed. He said that within five years, unless his group's demands were granted, they would burn the country down. Then he added that in his opinion the only thing that would save America would be a religious awakening. With that, at least, I agreed.

When President Eisenhower was in Pittsburgh in 1955 he said, "The history of free men is never really written by chance, but by choice—their choice." I believe that we have a choice; that our poverty problem, our race problem, the war problem, are problems of the heart, problems of the spirit. This is the basic crisis, and if we can solve the problem of the spirit, all our other problems can be solved. Therefore I believe it is time that we take our eyes off our shortcomings and off our failures and put them on Christ, who said, "You must be born again."

Eric Hoffer said the other night on television that we need a new birth. He was right: we do need a new birth. But it needs to start with somebody. It needs to start with me. It needs to start with you.

Christ said that you must be born again if you are to be saved. You must have a new birth, a new birth of the spirit, a new birth of the heart. And that could come about in your life today if you would be willing to get alone somewhere with God and say, "Oh, God, I have sinned against You. I put my trust and my confidence in Your Son, Jesus Christ." In that moment you can have a new birth, and through you, America and the world could have a new birth.

*Richard M. Nixon in*
Praying Hands

# Faith of a Nation

□ I have a closing comment on one additional point that I feel is closely related to our ability to achieve meaningful progress in human relationships. This point relates to the moral and spiritual posture of our society. We appear to be cutting loose from our Judeo-Christian concepts, with nothing else to tie up to. In some circles, it seems unfashionable to speak of God. . . .

I was considerably startled recently to hear the present day referred to as the "post-Christian era."

Personally, I cannot believe that faith in God in this nation is of so little depth. I suggest that if we really reflect on the matter we would hardly choose to live in a world without God—or have our children grow up and live in such a world. Further, I fear that in such a world there would be little hope of achieving the higher level of humanity that Mr. Franklin pleaded for back in 1780—and which should be our primary objective for the future.

On one occasion, during the tense deliberations surrounding the drafting of the Constitution, Mr. Franklin made this comment:

"In this situation of this assembly, groping in the dark as it were to find political truth, and scarce able to distinguish it when presented to us, how has it happened, sir, that we have not hitherto once thought of humbly applying to the Father of lights to illuminate our understanding?

"I have lived, sir, a long time, and the longer I live the more convincing proofs I see of this truth—that God governs in the affairs of men. And if a sparrow cannot fall to the ground without His notice, is it probable that an empire can rise without His aid?

"We have been assured, sir, in the Sacred Writings, that 'except the Lord build the house, they labour in vain that build it.' I firmly believe this; and I also believe that without His concurring aid, we shall succeed in this political building no better than the builders of Babel."

*From an address by Robert G. Dunlop,*
*President of Sun Oil Company,*
*before the Poor Richard Club,*
*Philadelphia*

# To the Business School Graduate

□ I hope you will always feel your responsibility both as a citizen and as a businessman. Far from being conflicting, the two roles are complementary. Each is self-supporting, but in their essentials they are inseparable. Ten to fifteen years ago the separation of private business and public affairs was a valid and workable premise; today it is no longer tenable. If free enterprise is to remain in the hands of men who lead society, the corporation will have to involve itself in more of the central concerns of society. Business today is exercising greater leadership than ever before in helping to solve major economic and social problems, but it will have to do even more in the future. This statement is not a response to the do-gooders; it is made because in business management are found resources, special skills and abilities, and above all the kind of leadership which must be brought to bear on these problems if we are to make significant headway toward their solution. Most young people in our colleges and universities have a high degree of social consciousness, and they have responded to social needs with energy and initiative. I hope this consciousness, as well as the initiative and energy that goes with it, will not be lost as you assume the responsibilities of families and careers.

A school can fill your cognitive bank with large deposits of knowledge: facts and ideas of all kinds. The bank can be well stocked with experience and with administrative skills. But how these resources will be applied when they are withdrawn from the bank depends to a large extent on your attitudes and personal values. Never forget that the ethics and moral values of the business community of tomorrow will be determined by you young men and women who are graduating from universities today. If the private enterprise system is to survive, there must have been instilled in you a belief that integrity, rooted in the bedrock of principle, is more important than operational competence.

*Ernest C. Arbuckle, Chairman of the Board,*
*Wells Fargo Bank, to the Graduate School of Business Administration*
*of the University of Michigan*

# Egotism

□ Egotism is the anesthetic that dulls the pain of stupidity.
*Frank Leahy in* Look Magazine

# The Responsibility of Parents

□ It is my judgment that too many of our fathers and mothers have abandoned too much of their responsibility to the school. These parents seem to feel that if they feed and clothe the child and provide him with a television set, the school should do everything else. The school is supposed to teach good manners, moral character, and patriotism along with history, mathematics, science, and all the other subjects that make up the stuff of education. All this is true. The school cannot overlook its duties in these matters, but it can be successful only if the parents realize that the home, when properly organized, is a far more potent educational unit than any school. The moral irresponsibility of many parents toward the education of their children is one of the truly terrifying developments of our time.

106

Since water rises no higher than its source, let us admit that too many American homes are as bare, intellectually and culturally, as Mother Hubbard's cupboard. If you say indignantly that this was not true of your homes when you were children, I am sure you are right. Otherwise, you would not now be here at Smith. But what I am concerned about is the great majority of homes whose daughters do not go to Smith—or Barnard.

A generation ago those homes had at least a few well-selected books and the children read them and re-read them. Today, too many of these homes rely for cultural sustenance upon the mass-media of radio, television, picture magazines, and the like. Do not misunderstand me, I have no quarrel with any of these newer means of communication and information. Their importance is undeniable. But in the home they should supplement and not replace good literature. And the indications are that in too many homes these mass-media instrumentalities are the culture piece de resistance and not the hors d'oeuvres. England has less than one-third of our population, and yet there are approximately three times as many book shops there as in our country. These figures speak for themselves. What they say is that American parents are not developing good reading habits in their children because the parents themselves are lacking in them.

We cannot disregard this criticism merely by replying that the current volume of production in books and periodicals is enormous. We have experienced in recent years an alarming increase in what could euphemistically be called trash, readily available at every corner drug store and newstand. Partially because of it, our standards of taste have become cheapened. Serious periodicals containing essays, interpretation, and opinion have dwindled almost to the vanishing point. They have been replaced by scores of other publications which, if accurately titled, would be called an "Introductory Guide to Juvenile Delinquency."

A part of our difficulty stems from the false assumption that genuine effort need not be required for the nourishment and development of a healthy, capable mind. We are so determined to make living easy, so determined to make the learning process painless, that we believe we have done all that is necessary when we reach for the terse summary of the news, the predigested article, the glossy photographs, and the channel selector of our television sets. Our fare must be encapsuled and sugarcoated. We admit that the body without adequate exercise becomes soft and flabby. We do not admit that our minds are subject to the same principles. . . .

The important point is to remember that there are very few more enduring pleasures than the possession of a well-furnished, well-exercised mind with a built-in intellectual curiosity that is insatiable.

*From an address by Dr. Grayson Kirk*
*at Smith College*

# Your Parents and Grandparents

□ This ceremony marks the completion of an important phase of your life. . . . But no one has more pride in your accomplishment than the next group I'd like to introduce to you. If you of the graduating class will look over into the bleachers to your right or left, I would like to introduce you to representatives of some of the most remarkable people ever to walk the earth. These are people you already know—your parents and grandparents. And remarkable they are indeed. Not long ago an educator from Northwestern University by the name of Bergan Evans got together some facts about these two generations. . . . These are the people who within just five decades have increased life expectancy by approximately 50 percent—who, while cutting the working day by a third, have more than doubled the per capita output. These are the people who have given you a healthier world than they found. And because of this you no longer have to fear epidemics of flu, typhus, diphtheria, smallpox, scarlet fever, measles, or mumps. And the dreadful polio is no longer a medical factor, while TB is almost unheard of. Let me remind you that these remarkable people lived through history's greatest depression. Many of these people know what it is to be poor, what it is to be hungry and cold.

And because of this, they determined that it would not happen to you, that you would have a better life, you would have food to eat, milk to drink, vitamins to nourish you, a warm house, better schools and greater opportunities to succeed. Because they gave you the best, you are the tallest, healthiest, brightest, and prob-

108

ably the best-looking generation to inhabit the land. Because they were materialistic, you will work fewer hours, learn more, have more leisure time, travel to more distant places, and have more of a chance to follow your life's ambition.

These are also the people who fought man's grisliest war. They are the people who defeated the tyranny of Hitler and who, when it was over, had the compassion to spend billions of dollars to help their former enemies rebuild their homelands. And these are the people who had the sense to begin the United Nations. It was representatives of these two generations who, through the highest court in the land, fought racial discrimination . . . to begin a new era of civil rights.

While they have done all these things, they have had some failures. They have not yet found an alternative for war, nor for racial hatred. . . . They have made more progress by the sweat of their brows than in any previous era—and don't you forget it. And, if your generation can make as much progress in as many areas as these two generations have, you should be able to solve a good many of the earth's remaining ills. It is my hope and I know the hope of these two generations that you find the answers to many of these problems that plague mankind. But it won't be easy. And you won't do it by negative thoughts, nor by tearing down or belittling. You can do it by hard work, humility, and faith in mankind.

*From an address delivered to*
*a recent graduating class by Dr. Eric Walker,*
*President, Pennsylvania State University*

# An Educated Person

☐ If you choose to work, you will succeed; if you don't you will fail.

If you neglect your work, you will dislike it; if you do it well, you will enjoy it.

If you join little cliques, you will be self-satisfied; if you make friends widely, you will be interesting.

If you gossip, you will be slandered; if you mind your own business, you will be liked.

109

If you act like a boor, you will be despised; if you act like a human being, you will be respected.

If you spurn wisdom, wise people will spurn you; if you seek wisdom, they will seek you.

If you adopt a pose of boredom, you will be a bore; if you show vitality, you will be alive.

If you spend your free time playing bridge, you will be a good bridge player; if you spend it in reading, discussing and thinking of things that matter, you will be an educated person.

*Sidney Smith, President, University of Toronto*

# The General Good

□ Let the general good be our yardstick on every great issue of our time. *Dwight Eisenhower*

# Distinguishing Characteristics in Our Lives

□ The United States ambassador to the Court of France wrote to George Washington concerning the king of that country: "In ordinary times he would have been a likeable and acceptable monarch. Unfortunately, his ancestors have bequeathed him a revolution."

These are not ordinary times in which we live. Things are not ordinary in China, Hong Kong, the Middle East, Viet Nam, or America. In a real sense we have been bequeathed a revolution! And ordinary citizenship, studentship, churchmanship, and Christian discipleship will not suffice. The ordinary citizen will be lost in the shuffle. Your ordinary student may not be around next semester. The ordinary churchman will be a drain on the fellowship. And the ordinary disciple will elicit a "ho-hum, so-what" from the world.

Our Lord did not so intend it! He once said, "I am come that you might have life and that you might have it more abundantly." The Scriptures also excite us with the promise, "Eye hath not seen, nor ear heard, neither have entered into the heart of man, the things which God hath prepared for them that love Him" (I Cor. 2:9).

Now, if these words are to come alive and if we are to be more than mere ordinary people in the midst of a revolution, there must be some distinguishing characteristics in our lives.

Let me suggest, first, that we need the *honesty of an open mind.*

We are a prejudiced breed of people. These prejudices show! We are highly opinionated about politics, education, sports, what we eat and wear, our culture and race and religion and our churches. Some of these prejudices we come by honorably and they are worthy. But others come because our minds are closed. For instance, a teacher in the classroom for more than forty years was asked to name the chief characteristic of the students through the years. Her answer was immediate, "His resistance to new ideas." In 1890 the United States Patent Office was petitioned that it be closed. Those signing the petition argued that everything worthwhile had already been invented! Newton spoke of his theory of gravitation, and people said it was an "insult to God." Galileo insisted that the earth rotated on its axis, and he was denounced. Fulton invented the steamboat, and it was dubbed "Fulton's Folly." Over in my home state of North Carolina at Kill Devil Hill, Kitty Hawk, two young men courageously guided a contraption called a flying machine a few feet above the sandy beaches. Back in their hometown in Ohio two men discussed the news of this adventure. One observed, "I don't believe it. God never intended for man to fly, and even if He had it wouldn't have been those Wright boys." In 1611, fifty-four scholars completed the translation of the King James Bible. They were called "heretics." And Mark Twain wrote to Walt Whitman on his seventieth birthday, congratulating him that he had lived through seventy of the greatest years of history. He then observed that the next thirty would see mankind rise to his full stature.

Now Christ met this resistance. Near the beginning of His public ministry the question was asked, "Can any good thing come out of Nazareth?" He was called a blasphemer, insurrectionist, the son of the devil, and a troublemaker. When they could no longer cope with His revolutionary concept of life they insisted, "Let him be crucified." The problem is not that Christianity has been tried and found dull, inconsistent and ineffective; the problem is that Christianity has not been tried!

The problem is not that Christianity is too difficult; the problem may be that it is too honest. Nearly forty years ago a missionary to the Philippines made two resolutions on New Year's Eve. He first resolved to experiment with the possibility of filling every minute with some thought of God. He then resolved to be as wide open toward people as he was toward God. The missionary then vowed, "I choose to make the rest of my life an experiment in this direction." As a result of this kind of commitment Frank Laubach has taught more than sixty million illiterates how to read. And all of this came because his mind was honestly open to God.

On the wall of an old English cathedral are these words:

> From the laziness that is content with half truth;
> From the cowardice that shrinks from new truth;
> From the arrogance that thinks it knows all truth,
> O God of Truth, deliver me!

We need the honesty of an open mind. We need also the discipline of a creative mind.

Jesus said, "Blessed are the meek. . . ." He was not speaking of the shy or the timid or the Casper Milquetoast variety of personality. Instead, He was referring to the man who is trained and disciplined. He was challenging man to let his mind be harnessed and controlled by God. In our churches we often speak of the stewardship of money and time and vocations. But what about the stewardship of mind? Psychologists tell us that we use about 5 percent of our mental capacity (some of your teachers may think this estimate is a little high!). What about the 95 percent, like an iceberg, that remains throughout life beneath the surface. This is why Thomas Edison said that genius is 5 percent brains and 95 percent work. This kind of discipline is seen in the life of Webster who spent thirty-six years compiling his first dictionary. At the time of his death he was working on another edition. Gibbon spent twenty years writing the *Rise and Fall of the Roman Empire*. Brahms took twenty years to write his first symphony. Sir Wm. Herschel, called by many the father of modern astronomy, tediously ground and polished the lens of his first telescope more than two hundred times. Bud Wilkinson, the former coach at Oklahoma University, once said, "The winning or losing is that intangible factor of mental toughness, without which one cannot be a winner." In order to win one must be willing to pay a greater price than his opponent. Some do not want to pay the price. We have no argument with them, we just don't want them around. All of this is why Hudson Taylor, a missionary, observed, "A man can be spiritually devoted, consecrated, dedicated, and of little use because his life is not disciplined."

Do you remember the first and the greatest commandment? Jesus said, "Thou shalt love the Lord thy God with all thy heart, and with all thy soul, and with all thy *mind.*" Again He said, "Take my yoke upon you and learn of me." And the apostle Paul writing to young Timothy urged him to "Stir up the gift." The potential is there! Stir it up! . . .

My favorite professor in college often said, "The soul of education is the education of the soul." With all of our emphasis on the academics (and this is worthy) we need to remember that when God measures a man He doesn't always put the tape around his head; often the tape is put around the man's heart! When the final lesson is learned and the last degree has been awarded, man must still bow in humility and confess that "life is bigger than I am, the infinite is greater than the finite, and God is greater than my thoughts." And again and again he will need to bow in reverence and quietly confess, "I don't know." This is why the greatest discoveries in life are among the "incomprehensibles," those things which cannot be analyzed or fully understood in the laboratory. This is also why Newton said that he felt like a child on the seashore, picking up a pebble of truth here and there, while out before him lay an ocean of undiscovered truth.

He came to Simpson College with a "gangling frame, a high falsetto voice, satchel full of poverty, and an insatiable desire to know everything." This is what they said of the tall, unlikely Negro student when he enrolled in college. George Washington Carver was the son of a slave and had known slavery himself. He was once traded for a horse valued at twenty-five dollars. He left Simpson College and enrolled at the University of Indiana and eventually secured his Ph.D. degree. He took a peanut and held it in his hand and prayed this prayer, "God, You made the peanut and You made me. Show me the mystery in this peanut." If you will check your encyclopedia you will find that more than two hundred products came out of this creative and prayerful adventure. Now, if the Lord God could take a Negro slave, once traded for a horse, and a peanut and accomplish this, I wonder what He could do with you and me if our hearts and minds were really bowed before Him!

"Eye hath not seen nor ear heard, neither have entered into the heart of man, the things which God hath prepared for them that love him."

Open your mind to God's truth. Discipline your mind... stretch it ... ask all of the questions you desire ... get all of the education you can ... but in the process don't forget to bow your mind.

*Excerpts from a high school address by the Reverend Bruce McIver, Dallas, Texas*

# What We Have in Common

☐ It is probably a pity that every citizen of each state cannot visit all the others, to see the differences, to learn what we have in common, and to come back with a richer, fuller understanding of America—in all its beauty, in all its dignity, in all its strength, in support of moral principle.    *Dwight Eisenhower*

# Part Three

---

## HUMOROUS STORIES

# Heaping

□ Home Economics Teacher: "When the sauce begins to boil, put in a tablespoon of water."
Sweet Young Thing: "Level or heaping?"

# Perfect Attendance

□ One teacher to another: "Not only is he the worst-behaving child in school, but he also has a perfect attendance record."

# To Impress Mother

□ A package of $100 bills was missing at the bank. The staff worked all night trying to locate them.

Next morning, Sally, a new clerk, walked into the bank to begin her daily duties.

An officer asked her, "Sally, did you see a package of $100 bills?"

"Oh, that," said Sally. "Why, I just took them home to show Mother the kind of work I'm doing."

# Her Turn

□ Said Mrs. Paul Revere: "I don't care who you say is coming, it's my night to use the horse!"

# Pessimist

□ A visitor, impressed by the beautiful campus and splendor of the buildings at a large university, turned to the professor showing him around and asked, "How many students have you here?"

The professor mused a moment and then answered, "Oh, I'd say about one in a hundred."

# Holding

□ Space age jargon has its advantages. Recently, a young woman closely connected with the space program was asked how old she'd be on her next birthday. Her reply—adapted from space shot language for an interrupted countdown—was: "Twenty-five and holding!"

# Correct

□ "Now, children," said the teacher, "I want you to write me an essay without a theme—just put down what is in you."

Ten minutes later Jimmy handed in the following:

"In me there is a heart, a lung, and an appendix. And then there is a stomach with two pieces of bread and butter, an apple, and five caramels."

# Heavy Losses

□ A small boy came hurriedly down the street and halted breathlessly in front of a stranger who was walking in the same direction. "Have you lost a dollar?" the boy asked.

"Yes, yes, believe I have!" said the stranger, feeling his pockets. "Have you found one?"

"Oh, no, I just wanted to find out how many have been lost today. Yours makes fifty-five."

# He Needed Help

□ An absentminded professor was straphanging in a bus. His left arm clasped a half-dozen bundles. He swayed to and fro. Slowly his face took on a look of alarm.

Noting this, a young man standing beside him said: "Can I help you, sir?"

"Yes," said the professor with relief. "Hold on to this strap while I get my fare out."

# Good Question

□ When a small boy approached a western TV star, the actor said, "Well, I suppose you'd like to have my autograph, wouldn't you, son?"

"No," replied the boy, "I was just wondering what you do with the horses after the cowboys get shot."

# Three Reasons

□ Filling out a series of reports at the end of the school year, one tired teacher came upon this line: "List three reasons for entering the teaching profession."

Without hesitation she filled in: (1) June, (2) July, (3) August.

# We Certainly Do

□ The principal of one high school whose nonteaching staff already included doctors, dentists, a psychologist, and a business manager was shocked to hear a member of his faculty suggest adding a handwriting expert.

"Handwriting analysis?" he snapped. "Ridiculous!"

"Who said anything about analyzing?" the teacher said wearily. "We just need somebody who can read it."

# Good Idea

□ A harried father was listening to his seven-year-old son scratch away on his violin, while the family dog howled an accompaniment.

After a few minutes of the dissonant practice session, the father asked the son: "Can't you play something the dog doesn't know?"

# Better Help Him Now

□ Wife to reluctant husband, who is helping their small son with his homework.

"Help him now while you can. Next year he goes into the fourth grade."

# Better but Not Good

□ "How are your children doing at school?" asked a friend.

"Better," replied the other, "but I still go to PTA meetings under an assumed name."

# Good Memory

□ Smith: "You remember Jim Barrington?"
Brown: "Yes, what's his name?"
Smith: "How should I know?"

# Late Arrival

□ Two boys were taking their first airplane trip and were quite impressed at the beginning. But about halfway in the trip, the pilot's voice came over the intercom: "The Number 1 engine is out, but the other three will carry us safely into Los Angeles. We will be ten minutes late."

In another few minutes came this message: "The Number 2 engine is on fire. We will arrive safely in Los Angeles, twenty minutes late."

A little later they heard: "Our Number 3 engine just fell off. Bear with us. We will reach out destination one hour late."

At this, one of the boys turned to the other and said, "Boy, I sure hope we don't lose Number 4! We'll be up here all day!"

# Well Known

□ A boy sought a job in a drugstore.

"Your name?" asked the druggist.

"Patrick Henry."

"That's a pretty well-known name, isn't it?"

"It ought to be," the boy replied. "I've been delivering groceries around this neighborhood for two years."

# He Got Even

□ "What's the new halfback's name?" asked the coach.

"Osscowinsinsiski," replied his assistant.

"Good," exclaimed the coach with satisfaction. "Put him on the first team. Boy, will I get even with those newspaper sports-writers now!"

# Salesmanship

□ The big shot sales manager was approached by six little Girl Scouts peddling cookies. "Why do you want to see me?" he asked.

"Because you are so handsome," smiled one little girl.

He bought twelve boxes and went back to his desk murmuring, "There are no brighter sales tools than truth and honesty."

# Education

□ The professor of mathematics and his fiancee were out roaming in the fields when she plucked a daisy and looking roguishly at him, she began to pull off the petals, saying, "He loves me, he loves me not—."

"You are giving yourself a lot of unnecessary trouble," said the professor. "You should count up the petals, and if the total is an even number the answer will be in the negative; if an uneven number, in the affirmative."

# Point of View

□ When the other fellow takes a long time to do something, he's slow; when you take a long time, you're thorough. When he doesn't do something, he's lazy; when you don't, you're too busy. When he succeeds, he's lucky; when you do, you deserve it.

# Good at Track

□ As the band instructor approached him, the high school trumpet player said worriedly, "What's the matter? Didn't I do all right in the parade today?"

"Sure, you did fine," the instructor replied. "You won by at least a yard."

# Simple

□ "One trouble with modern society is that we are too specialized. Now, I happen to have a good background in the liberal arts, but I must confess that I haven't the faintest idea of how the TV works," admitted the youth.

"My goodness!" exclaimed the wide-eyed co-ed. "It's awful easy. You just turn the knobs and you see the picture.

# Correct

☐ Deep lies the drift across the drive; I know what must be done.
I bravely grasp the shovel—and hand it to my son.

# Good Reason

☐ Mother: "Jimmy, sit down and I'll tell you a story."
Jimmy: "I can't sit down 'cause I just told Daddy one."

# Valuable Inscription

☐ Little Timothy had bought Grandma a Bible for Christmas and
wanted to write a suitable inscription on the flyleaf. He racked his
brain until suddenly he remembered that his father had a book
with an inscription of which he was very proud. So Tim decided to
copy it.

Imagine Grandma's surprise on Christmas morning when she
opened her gift, a beautiful Bible, and found inscribed the following phrase: "To Grandma, with the compliments of the Author."

# Short Story

☐ Slippery ice—very thin; pretty girl—tumbled in; saw a fellow—on the bank; gave a shriek—then she sank; boy on hand—
heard her shout; jumped right in—pulled her out; now he's hers—
very nice; but she had—to break the ice.      *Evans Echoes*

# How Nice 'Twould Be!

☐ How nice 'twould be if knowledge grew on bushes as the berries
do; then we would plant our spelling seed, and gather all the words

we need! And sums from off our slates we'd wipe and wait for figures to be ripe, and go into the field and pick whole bushels of arithmetic!

Or, if we wished to learn Chinese, we'd just go out and shake the trees, and grammar, then, in all our towns would grow with proper verbs and nouns; and in the garden there would be great bunches of geography, and all the passersby would stop and marvel at the knowledge crop! *Sunshine Magazine*

# Most Popular

□ Grandfather was having a chat with Junior. "Tell me, Junior," he said, "who is the most popular boy in your school?"

Junior thought for a moment. "I guess it's Bill Jones. Last term he gave us all the measles."

# New Job

□ Myrtle: "I didn't know you were on the football team. What do you do?"

Herman: "I'm an aerialist."

Myrtle: "An aerialist?"

Herman: "Yes, I keep the footballs blown up."

# Would You Believe It?

□ A study by the American Council on Education involved asking freshmen entering sixty-one colleges what careers they hoped to follow. Here are some of the choices as written by the various students:

"Business," "Buseness," "Finnace," "Holesaid Salisman," "Denestry," "Physist," "Technction," "Airnotics," "Treacher," "Stewardes," "Secteral," "Engenering."

One other was "undesided," while another was "undecieded." And these comments came from nondropouts!

# Direct Hit

□ The big-game hunter took his wife on his newest safari. The sportsman had bagged a few minor trophies, but the great prize was the head of a huge lion, killed by his wife.

"What did she hit it with?" asked a friend admiringly. "That .303 Magnum rifle you gave her?"

"No," answered her husband, dryly, "with the station wagon we rented!"

# The Twelve Days

□ On the fifth day of April, my true love gave to me—five packs of seed, four bags of peat, three bags of fertilizer, two bottles of insect spray, and a pruning knife for the pear tree.

# TV

□ The lady of the house summoned a TV serviceman to fix the set. Spreading out his tools, the repairman inquired: "What seems to be the trouble?"

Replied the little woman: "Well, for one thing, all the programs are lousy."

# Traffic Lights

□ A lady who was a rather poor driver stalled her car at traffic signals which were against her. As the green flashed on, her engine stalled again, and when she had restarted it the light was again red.

This flustered her so much that when green returned she again stalled her engine and the cars behind began to blow their horns. While she was waiting for the green the third time, the policeman on duty stepped over to the car and with a smile said: "Those are the only colors we have today, madam."

# Was That Nice?

□ Little Johnnie had to stand in the corner at school for putting mud in a little girl's mouth.

His mother was horrified when she heard about it. "Why in the world did you put mud in Margaret's mouth?"

"Well," said Johnnie, shrugging his shoulders, "it was open."

# Good Reason

□ Beggar, running up to a man on the sidewalk: "Quick, can you spare a dime?"

Man: "Sure, but what's your hurry?"

Beggar: "I'm double-parked."

# Description

□ Girl: "What position do you play on the basketball team this season?"

Bench Warmer: "Oh, sort of crouched and bent over."

# History

□ A fifth-grader turned in the following essay on history: "It was Nathan Haley who said: 'I regret that I have but one life to give for my country.' This has come to be known as Haley's comment."

# Helpful

□ "Sir, can you help a man in trouble?"

"Sure. What kind of trouble do you want to get in?"

# Misquoting

□ There are many stories of children misquoting the Lord's Prayer. A little girl was heard praying: "And lead me not into Penn Station." And a small boy gave this version: "Howard be Thy name."

Another youngster said; "Our Father who art in heaven, how did You know my name?"

# Mathematics

□ Bill: "Shall I cut this pie into six or eight pieces?"

Jim: "Better cut it in six—I don't think I can eat all eight pieces."

# Lost

□ Two Boy Scouts were on a hike. One said to the other: "Speaking for myself, I'm trustworthy, loyal, helpful, courteous, kind, obedient, cheerful, thrifty, brave, clean—and lost!"

# Good Fit

□ Said the sergeant to the recruit: "How does the new uniform fit?"

"The pants are all right, but I'd be afraid to run in this jacket for fear my feet would get tripped up in the pockets."

# Gave Up

□ A Frenchman was relating his experience in learning the English language. "When I discovered that if I was quick I was fast," he said, "and that if I was tied I was fast, if I spent too freely I was fast, and that not to eat is to fast, I was discouraged. But when I came across the sentence, 'The first one won one one-dollar prize,' I gave up trying to learn the English language."

## Sorry He Asked

□ "Which way to Rock Ridge?" asked a motorist of a dejected-looking man perched on a fence near a ramshackle farmhouse.

The native languidly waved his hand toward the right.

"Thanks," said the motorist. "How far is it?"

"'Tain't so very far," was the drawling reply. "When you get there, you'll wish it was a lot farther."

## Economic Definitions

□ A professor of finance at Stanford University, Dr. Theodore Kreps, has simplified the entire subject of economics with these three basic definitions: Recession—when the man next door to you loses his job; Depression—when you lose your job; Panic—when your wife loses her job.

## Cured Her

□ Jones: "Has your son's college education been of any value?"

Smith: "Oh, yes, it cured his mother of bragging about him."

## The Wilderness

□ The trouble with most people these days is that they want to reach the Promised Land without going through the wilderness.

*Survey Bulletin*

# Perceptive Student

☐ "John, what animal is peculiar to Australia?" asked the teacher.
"An elephant, sir."
"An elephant! Elephants aren't found in Australia."
"That's right, that's why it would be peculiar."

# To the Head of the Class

☐ The professor of chemistry was giving a demonstration of the properties of various acids.
"Now," he said, "I am going to drop this dime into this glass of acid. Will it dissolve?"
"No, sir," replied one of the students.
"No?" said the demonstrator. "Then perhaps you will explain to the class why it won't dissolve."
"Because," came the answer, "if it did you wouldn't drop it in."

# Satisfied

☐ Worried over what to give his girl for her birthday, a boy asked his mother for help. "Mom," he said, "if you were going to be sixteen years old tomorrow, what would you want?"
Her heartfelt reply was: "Not another thing!"

# Punctuation

☐ A college English professor wrote the words "woman without her man is a savage" on the board, directing the students to punctuate it correctly. He found that the males looked at it one way, the females another:
The males wrote: "Woman, without her man, is a savage!"
The females wrote: "Woman! Without her, man is a savage."

## Not Shy

□ "I'm afraid your little brother is shy," said the hostess at a birthday party. "He hasn't moved from that one place all afternoon."

"No, ma'am," explained the boy's elder sister, "he's not shy. It's just that he's never had a necktie on before, and he thinks he's tied to something."

## Discipline

□ The small boy had been mischievous and his mother's patience was exhausted. She made ready to spank him but he hid under a bed upstairs. His mother could not get him out and so left him until her husband came home. The father said, "Leave him to me." He went upstairs and gently raised the bedspread. To his surprise he was greeted by his son with, "Hello, Dad. Is she after you too?"

## Acoustics

□ The visiting preacher was being shown the church by the warden who warned him that the congregation had difficulty in hearing because, he said, the agnostics in the church were terrible.

## Repartee

□ A biologist with a one-track mind was seated at dinner next to a lady and engaged her in discussion on the subject of ants. He sought in his enthusiasm to impress her, and said, "And do you know, they even have their own army and their own police force!"

"Indeed," she replied, "but no navy?"

# Tact

□ A mother was reading to her small son while his brother aged ten stood by listening.

"There is a grey hair in your head, Mama," he exclaimed.

"Pluck it out, please," she replied.

He did so and as he handed it to her he said, "One of your mother's I think."

# It Worked

□ Johnny had been to a friend's birthday party and was telling his mother all about it. "And I hope," said his mother, "that you didn't ask for a second piece of cake?" "Oh no!" he replied, "I asked Mrs. Brown for the recipe so that you could make one for me and she gave me two extra pieces without my asking at all."

# Dared Him

□ Tom's birthday party was being arranged and his mother urged him particularly to ask Billie, a boy with whom he did not get on very well at school. The party went well but Billie did not attend. Afterwards Tom's mother said to him, "I wonder why Billie didn't come—you did invite him, didn't you?" "Of course I did," he replied, "but then I dared him to come."

# Absentminded Professor

□ An absentminded professor was observed walking with one foot continually in the gutter and the other on the pavement. A friend who met him stopped to talk and inquired how he was. "Well," he replied, "quite well, until about ten minutes ago. Since then I have been limping."

# A Great Strain

□ The lecturer in an English University was taking his students through *The Merchant of Venice*. At the speech beginning "the quality of mercy is not strained," a question was asked about the word *strained;* was it used in the sense that a muscle was strained or in the sense that tea was strained through a strainer? The lecturer was baffled. He looked intently at his text. Then suddenly his face relaxed and he replied in triumph, "But it said it is *not* strained—so the question doesn't arise!"

# Grammar

□ I can manage the first two Articles
"A" or "An" and sometimes "The"
But the "Nouns," the Pronouns Particles
Verbs and Adverbs Partickle me.
Nouns I know are common and proper
They've got number gender and case,
But on the Verbs I come a cropper,
Rhyme or reason I can't trace.

Take a Verb now as an example,
You'd say rightly drink, drank, drunk,
But on the rules of Grammar you'd trample
If with your eyes you blink, blank, blunk.
Sink, sank, sunk is right by Lennie,
But you can hardly think, thank, thunk,
Murray for you would be one too many,
If at a girl you wink, wank, wunk.

*Leslie Missen*

# The Professor's Umbrella

□ The professor was absentminded and mislaid everything. One day he returned home without his umbrella, and his wife tried to get some idea from him of where to look for it. "Tell me," she said, "precisely when did you first miss it?" "My dear," he replied, "it was when I put my hand up to let it down after a sharp shower."

# Professor to Student

□ "Your speech has exhausted time and encroached upon eternity."

# Getting Ready for His Career

□ Two coworkers were discussing the fact that they both had youngsters who were away at college. "What does your boy plan to be when he graduates?" asked one man.

"I'm not really sure, but judging from the letters he writes home, I'd say he was going to be a professional fund raiser."

# Congratulations

□ I liked the straightforward way in which you dodged the issues.

# It Was Once

□ A rather frail man was looking for a job and applied at a Canadian logging camp. The large and burly foreman took one look at him and said, "You are not big enough and strong enough to work in a logging camp."

The man replied, "Just give me a chance. Let me show you."

So they got him an ax which was about as big as he was.

He said, "Which tree shall I cut down?" and they pointed out a tremendous fir tree probably a hundred feet high.

He dragged the ax over and in no time had the tree down. The foreman could not believe what he had seen.

He said, "Where did a man who weighs about a hundred pounds and is only five feet tall learn how to cut a tree down so rapidly?"

The man replied, "I have had a great deal of experience, but the best experience I ever had was in the Sahara forest.

The foreman said, "The Sahara forest? I thought the Sahara was a desert."

The man said, "Yes, it is now!"

# Not Much of a Truck Driver

□ A truck driver was sitting all by himself at the counter of the Neverclose Restaurant. The waitress had just served him when three swaggering, leather-jacketed motorcyclists came in, apparently spoiling for a fight. One grabbed the hamburger off his plate; another took a handful of his French fries; and the third picked up his coffee and began to drink it. The trucker did not respond as one might expect. Instead, he calmly rose, picked up his check, walked to the front of the room, put the check and his half-dollar on the cash register, and went out the door. The waitress followed him to put the money in the till and stood watching out the window as he drove off. When she returned, one of the cyclists said to her: "Well, he's not much of a man, is he?" She replied, "Nope. He's not much of a truck driver either—he just ran over three motorcycles."

# Small Meeting

□ Small boy to his father: "I'm supposed to tell you there's going to be a small Parent Teachers Association meeting tomorrow night."

"Well, if it's going to be a small one, do I have to go?" asked the father.

"Oh, yes," answered the son. "It's just you, me, and the principal."

# Classified Advertisement

□ Will exchange evening gown worn only once at a ball, for a perambulator.

# Making Money

□ "I feel sure, my poor man," said the sympathetic old lady, visiting a federal prison, "it was poverty that brought you to do this."

"No, ma'am, quite the contrary," replied the prisoner. "I happened to be coining money."

# Written Comments of Students on a Story

□ "It has many points of intrest."
"Very intresting"
"Real intrested"
"Very intersting"

# Seems Logical

□ After listening to a lengthy lecture from his father about his sloppy appearance, long hair, straggly beard, and general attitude, the teen-ager blurted out: "But, Dad, I gotta be a nonconformist. . . . How else can I be like the other kids?"

# Deficit

□ High school teacher: "Explain the meaning of *deficit*."
Freshman: "Deficit is what you've got when you haven't got as much as you had, when you had nothing."

# Don't Ask Foolish Questions

□ A small boy leading a donkey passed by an army camp. A couple of soldiers wanted to have some fun with the lad.

"What are you holding onto your brother so tight for, sonny?" said one of them.

"So he won't join the army," the youngster replied without blinking an eye.

# Only a Small Rattle

□ Professor: "Why don't you answer me?"

Student: "I did, professor. I shook my head."

Professor: "But you don't expect me to hear it rattle way up here, do you?"

# Bigoted

□ Asked how she liked her new boss, a young secretary remarked: "Oh, he's not bad, only he's kind of bigoted."

"How do you mean?"

"Well," she explained, "he thinks words can be spelled only one way."

# He Knew

□ *A Diplomatic Tale:* At a recent Kremlin reception for the ambassador from the Communist puppet state of Mongolia, the scene was set for the official toasts. However, an interpreter was not to be found, so one of the guests, a Polish professor from Warsaw, volunteered to handle the interpretation. Soviet Premier Kosygin delivered a toast in Russian and then the Mongolian ambassador stepped forward. He paused after each sentence and the Polish professor translated into Russian as follows:

"His Excellency says that he is happy to be in the heartland of socialism. . . .

"His Excellency said he is proud and happy to be at the center of the anti-imperialist struggle. . . .

"His Excellency says that the people of Mongolia will stand with the forces of liberation throughout the world. . . ."

After the professor concluded, a friend commented with surprise, "I didn't realize you knew Mongolian." "I don't," the professor whispered, "but I knew what the ambassador would say."

# No Real Choice

□ Wife to husband: "Shall we watch the 5:30 news and get indigestion, or wait for the 10:00 o'clock news and have insomnia?"

# Exaggeration

□ Australian proudly showing his farm to a Texan: "How do you like the size of these oranges?"

Texan: "In Texas we have them as big as grapefruits."

Farmer: "How do you like the size of these cantaloupes?"

Texan: "In Texas we have them as big as watermelons."

Just then a kangaroo comes hopping by and the Australian says, "Now, don't tell me that you have grasshoppers bigger than this, too."

# Worried

□ Two young recruits were being interviewed for the Navy and were asked: "Do you know how to swim?"

They both looked puzzled and then one of them replied: "What's the matter? Aren't there enough ships?"

# Naturally

◻ Teacher: "Why don't you bring back your report card?"

Junior: "You gave me an 'A' in something and they're still mailing it to relatives."

# It Isn't Easy

◻ A father was telling a friend how he finally cured his seventeen-year-old son of habitually being late to school:

"I bought him a car."

"But how did that help?"

"Well," replied the father, "he has to get going an hour earlier to find a place in the school parking lot."

# Smart Boy

◻ Art: "Name two pronouns."

Ted: "Who, me?"

# The Good Old Days

◻ Many persons seem to agree with the spirit of the Old French Proverb "Ah, for the good old days—when we were so unhappy."

# Modern American

◻ A modern American has been described as a person who drives a bank-financed car over a bond-financed highway on credit card gas to open a charge account at a department store so he can fill his savings-and-loan financed home with installment-purchased furniture.

# Tough Spot

□ "I'm in a tough spot," the small boy said to his mother. "The teacher said I must write more legibly, and if I do she will find out I can't spell."

# Father Takes It

□ Discussing family problems, one father remarked to the other, "I finally stopped arguing with my teen-age son about borrowing the car. Now, whenever I want it, I just take it!"

# Not Wasted

□ Teen-ager pointing to crumpled fender on family car, "Great news, Dad, you haven't been pouring those insurance payments down the drain."

# Food for Thought

□ If you want to sing while you
    drive along the highway:
At 50 miles per hour, sing:
"Highways are Happyways."
At 60 miles per hour, sing:
"I am but a stranger here,
    Heaven's my home."
At 70 miles per hour, sing:
"Nearer my God to Thee."
At 80 miles per hour, sing:
"When the roll is called up yonder,
    I'll be there."
At 90 miles and up, sing;
    "Lord, I'm Coming Home."

# How to Bring Happiness

◻ If you want to bring happiness to a loved one, repeat one of these phrases: (1) I love you. (2) Dinner is ready. (3) All is forgiven. (4) Sleep until noon. (5) Keep the change. (6) Here's that $10.

# Very Careful

◻ A careful driver approached a railway crossing. He stopped his car, looked carefully, and listened. All he heard was the car behind him crashing into his back bumper.

# Accuracy

◻ It is odd how different people hearing the same thing get entirely different meanings from it. Three newsmen listened to a conversation between a man and his wife in the next room. When asked to guess what they'd heard, one said they were talking about the zoo because he heard the words, "trained deer." The second said it was about traveling because he'd heard the words, "Find out about the train, dear." The third claimed the subject was music—he heard "trained ear." When they asked the lady what she'd asked her husband, she said she had asked him if it had "rained here last night."

# That Crazy English Language

◻ A stranger in our land was he; he tried to learn our spelling. He thought it would as easy be as buying or as selling. He tried to write, but couldn't quite learn when to wright or right. He could not tell just where he stood, when using cood or wood or shood. He had to stand a lot of chaffing, when cruel people started laffing. Then other things confused him so, as doe and dough and roe and row, and mail and male and sail and sale, and many more that turned him pail. Said he, "I left my wife and daughter in other lands across the waughter; I wanted much to bring them here, but they will have to stay, I fere, and I must leave you." With a sigh he added, "Else I'll surely digh."

## Is That Better?

□ Mother: "Johnny, did I hear you call your sister a silly old thing? Say you're sorry."

Johnny: "I'm sorry you're a silly old thing."

## Identity

□ As all the children of a large family scrambled into the back of the family station wagon, one of them called out, "Whose foot am I sitting on?"

"If it has a brown sock," came the reply, "it's mine."

## Said Nothing

□ "What did Tarzan say when he saw the elephants coming over the hill with wrap-around sunglasses on?"

"I don't know, what?"

"Nothing—he didn't recognize them!"

## Not Too Hard

□ A teen-ager drove into a gas station and said, "I'll take a quart of gas and a half pint of oil."

"Do you want me to sneeze in your tires also?"

# He Knows Not

□ He who knows not and knows he knows not, knows a lot. He who knows not and knows not he knows not, knows not!

# Easier

□ Dick, aged three, did not like soap and water. One day, his mother was trying to reason with him. "Surely you want to be a clean little boy, don't you?"

"Yes," tearfully agreed Dick, "but can't you just dust me?"

# That's Different

□ "So you think you should have a raise?" the boss bellowed. "I suppose you have often thought what you would do if you had my income, haven't you?"

His faithful clerk smiled wryly.

"No, sir," he replied, "but I have often wondered what you would do if you had mine!"

# Honesty

□ Two horse traders engaged in a rather bitter discussion. Said one, "That horse you sold me is almost blind."

"Well," replied the other, "remember I told you he was a fine horse but that he didn't look good."

# Simple

□ An Eskimo won a trip to New York as a prize for catching the most seals in season. When he returned home, he brought with him a length of pipe, which he set up in his igloo so it protruded through the roof.

His wife asked what it was for.

"That's a trick I learned in New York," he replied. "When you want more heat, you bang on this pipe."

# Either Way

□ School Board Member: Do you teach that the world is round or flat?

Teacher Applicant: With my years of training, I can teach it either way.

# Possibilities

□ Bureaucrat: "If we are unable to figure out a way to spend $300 million, we'll be out of jobs."

Secretary: "How about building a bridge across the Mississippi?"

Bureaucrat: "That won't cost $300 million."

Secretary: "Lengthwise?"

# A Sense of Humor

□ A friend of mine in the ministry was surprised one Sunday when he read his morning worship bulletin. Following the sermon were the words in parentheses, "Congregation will be seated for medication."

It is said that Dr. Harry Emerson Fosdick, the eminent clergyman of a quarter century ago, glanced at his printed morning worship service to find that the hymn prior to the sermon included the directions, "Congregation standing." The title of Dr. Fosdick's sermon was "What Are You Standing For?"

A man slipped on some ice. An instant later, a lady fell and landed in his lap. Together they slid down a slight incline. The man said politely, "I'm sorry, madam, I get off here." A good laugh followed.

To be able to laugh, especially at one's self, is a necessary attribute. Blessed is the man who does not take himself too seriously.

*The Reverend Harleigh Rosenberg*
*in* Sunshine Magazine

# That Proves It

□ The day before a big college game a bombshell burst on the coach with the dean's announcement that the star player had been disqualified. The coach hurried to the dean to ask why.

The dean said, "We caught him cheating yesterday."

"I don't believe my player would cheat," the coach blustered. "What evidence do you have?"

"The star athlete sat right across from the star student. When their exam papers were compared, it was found the two were identical on the first nine questions."

"But," said the coach, "that doesn't prove anything. Maybe the player crammed."

"I can answer that best," said the dean, "by the manner in which they replied to the last question. The A student wrote: 'I don't know.' The player wrote: 'I don't know either.' "

# Make It Short

□ An African tribe has a fine method of dealing with public speakers which might well be used in this country. This tribe considers long speeches injurious both to the orator and his audience. To protect both there is an unwritten law that every public speaker must stand on one foot while addressing his hearers. As soon as his other foot touches the ground his speech is brought to a close, by force if necessary.

# After-Dinner Speech

□ When Daniel got into the lions' den and looked around he thought to himself, "Whoever's got to do the after-dinner speaking, it won't be me."

# Reasonable

□ An eight-year-old girl was showing her preschool sister a picture of Mary and the baby Jesus. The younger girl examined the picture closely and then asked, "Where's Joseph?"

The older sister thought for a moment and then replied, "He's taking the picture."

# They're Both Bad!

□ That dimwit driver streaking by—it's hard to tell if gal or guy. But when it comes to causing wrecks, I doubt it matters 'bout the sex!

# The Teacher's Prayer

□ Two men went to church to pray. One was a man named Babbitt and the other a teacher.

And the man named Babbitt stood and looking into the eyes of heaven, exclaimed:

"O Lord, I thank Thee that I am not like these professional men, even as this poor school teacher. I pay half the preacher's salary; it is my money that built this church; I subscribe liberally to foreign missions, and to all the work of the church. It is my money that advanceth Thy cause."

But the school teacher bowed himself in humility and said:

"O God, be merciful unto me. I was that man's teacher."

# Lots of Trouble

□ Two men stopped each other on the street. The hectic nature of their business worlds was the subject of conversation. One said, "You sure look worried."

"Man," said the other, "I've got so many troubles that if anything happens today, it will be at least two weeks before I can worry about it."

# Only Exposed

□ The father was down at the college having a little visit with his son. One evening he met one of the professors his son had had in a course.

"I'm delighted to meet you. My son took math under you last year, didn't he?"

"Pardon me," said the professor. "He was exposed to it but he didn't take it."

# A Bag of Wind

□ The coach of a famous football team had been called upon to give an after-dinner speech to a group of business men. He attempted to apply his coaching rules to life in general and in conclusion he was heard to proclaim:

"After all is said and done, it pays to use football tactics in this world. Look how nicely a football sails along; and all it is is a bag of wind with a stiff front."

# A Devoted Baseball Fan

□ Lyndon Johnson, on the trials of being a devoted Senator fan: "I do all I can for them. I even pray for the team each night. I hope the Supreme Court doesn't declare that unconstitutional."

# Why

□ General Dwight Eisenhower, asked if he noticed anything different about his golf game since he left the White House: "Yes, a lot more golfers beat me."

# Plenty of Advice

□ Governor John Connally, addressing Texas high school coaches: "You're the only group of people who gets more advice on how to run your business than we elected public officials do."

# Difficult Choice

□ Tallulah Bankhead, incurable Giant fan: "There have been only two geniuses in the world—Willie Mays and Willie Shakespeare. But, dahling, I think you'd better put Shakespeare first."

# Unlucky

□ Duffy Daugherty, Michigan State football coach: "My only feeling about superstition is that it's unlucky to be behind at the end of a game."

# Very Sensitive

□ When little Percival arrived at school on the opening day, he carried the following note to the teacher:

"Dear Teacher: Our sweet little Percival is a very delicate, nervous child, and if he is naughty—and he is likely to be naughty at times—just punish the boy next to him, and that will frighten him so he'll be good."

# A Team Effort

☐ Bob Walters, La Salle basketball coach, on his team's thirty-one point upset loss to Duquesne: "I can't say any one player caused this. It honestly was a team effort."

# Making a Speech

☐ Ladies and Gentlemen—and the rest of you—good, bad, and indifferent: The only thing that I know to say just now is the little girl's prayer who was called at six o'clock in the morning: "Oh Lord, how I hate to get up."

# Free Admission

☐ A little tot in church for the first time watched the ushers pass the offering plates. When they neared the pew where he sat, the youngster piped up so that everyone could hear, "Don't pay for me, Daddy; I'm under five."

# Identity Clear

☐ Roosevelt Grier, 300-pound Los Angeles Ram tackle, on being asked if he had a middle initial: "No, but I've never been mistaken for anyone else."

# When Things Go Wrong

☐ When things go wrong, as they sometimes will, when the road you're trudging seems all uphill; when funds are low and debts are high, and you want to smile, but you sit and sigh; when care is pressing you down a bit, rest, if you must, but don't you quit!

# Take Your Choice

□ Two counterfeiters whose printing press went haywire and turned out $18 bills took them back into the hills in the hope of finding ignorant people who would exchange them for good currency. They found a little country store with a bewhiskered old gentleman sitting on the porch. They asked if he had change for an $18 bill.

The old man never batted an eye as he said, "How do you want it—three sixes or two nines?"

# Didn't Know Too Many Words

□ Sid Gillman, San Diego Charger coach, on one of his rookies: "He doesn't know the meaning of the word 'fear.' Of course, there are lots of other words he doesn't know either."

# Hush

□ Hush, little snowflake, don't you cry; you'll be a dewdrop next July!

# On the Subway

□ I rose and gave her my seat; I could not let her stand—she made me think of my mother, with that strap held in her hand.

# Record

□ Young secretary to prospective employer: "I'm not a very good typist—but I can erase sixty words a minute."

# Life Story

☐ The evolution of a man's ambitions:
To be a circus clown.
To be like Dad.
To be a fireman.
To do something noble.
To get wealthy.
To make ends meet.
To get the old-age pension.

# Time to Wash Up

☐ Between the dark and the daylight, when the night is beginning to lower, little paws, black from the day's occupations, make what is known as the "Children's Scour!"

# Hopeful?

☐ A schoolteacher was trying to explain subtraction to his young pupils.

"You have ten fingers," he said. "Suppose you had three less fingers, what would you have?"

A girl gave the quick answer, "I'd have no music lesson."

# Not Easy

☐ Centerville (Ohio) High School's seniors had a sublime send-off at graduation exercises.

After diplomas were granted, a senior girl rose and solemnly said:

"Now, will you please rise for the benediction and continue rising while the class sings our alma mater."

# Space Age

□ If you read to a small boy these days the nursery rhyme about the cow jumping over the moon, he asks, "How could a cow have that much thrust?"

# Turn Backward

□ Backward, turn backward, O Time, in your flight, and tell me just one thing I studied last night!

# It Ain't Good

□ In a Parisian sidewalk cafe, the American tourist gave his order with glib assurance. Not wishing to be thought a show-off, he turned to his companion and said modestly, "My high school French ain't so good maybe, but I make myself understood."

The waiter hesitated for a second, and then with a barely perceptible bow, he murmured, "If you don't mind my saying so, sir, it compares favorably with your high school English."

*Ivern Boyett,* Wall Street Journal

# Public Speaking

□ As the speaker was giving the main address, a fellow in the back put his hand to his ear and said, "Louder."

The speaker raised his voice, but the fellow continued to say "Louder."

Finally, a man down front couldn't stand it and yelled at the man in the back, "What's the matter, can't you hear him?"

"No," said the other fellow.

"Well," said the man down front, "Move over, I'm coming back to sit with you."

# Close

☐ Professor: "How far are you from the correct answer?"
Student: "Two seats."

# Helpful

☐ The youngster came home after his first day at school.
"What happened?" asked his mother.
"Nothing," he replied with a shrug. "Except a lady wanted to know how to spell cat, and I told her."

# Right

☐ Teacher: "Name three collective nouns."
Pupil: "Dustpan, wastebasket, and vacuum cleaner."

# Cruel

☐ A family of bears, rummaging in a Yellowstone National Park garbage dump, looked up when a car crammed with eight tourists pulled up at the side of the road.
"Isn't it cruel," commented Papa Bear to his brood, "to keep them caged up like that?"

# Simple

☐ An excited citizen rushed into the FBI office, waving a little black notebook. "I found this on the elevator," he shouted, "it's in code!"
The local FBI agent examined it and read: "K1, P2, CO8" etc.

Putting the intricate code-breaking system to work, he found he couldn't break the code. He sent it to Washington for expert attention.

The young clerk quickly decoded it as follows: "Knit one, purl two, cast on eight."

# Part Four

---

## INTERESTING
## ILLUSTRATIONS
## FROM
## INTERESTING LIVES

# Abraham Lincoln

▢ Certain distinctive features of Lincoln's style reflect his limited frontier heritage. According to his own testimony, he attended school "by littles." In preparing an autobiography for partisan purposes on the eve of the 1860 canvass, he concluded that the "agregate [which he misspelled] of all his schooling did not amount to one year." John Hanks testified that he kept Aesop's Fables and the Bible "always within reach" and that he read them again and again. Years later Billy Herndon, his law partner, said that these works "furnished him with the many figures of speech and parables which he used with such happy effect. . . ." Herndon, who was something of an intellectual, said that "Lincoln read less and thought more than any man in America." Herndon should have made an exception of newspapers, however, for Lincoln was an avid newspaper reader, much to the annoyance of Mrs. Lincoln who once complained because still another miserable paper was added to those already tossed upon her doorstep. In later years, Lincoln read Shakespeare: *King Lear, Richard the Third, Hamlet,* and especially *Macbeth.*

*From an address by Robert G. Gunderson*

# Penetrating Beyond Our Walls

▢ I was ready to tuck the children into bed. As I went over to open the window I noticed the next door neighbor was practicing the piano. I could hear his music clearly though I knew his windows were closed. It had never occurred to me that perhaps my own practicing penetrated beyond my walls. The most amazing walls are penetrated. We go back hundreds of years and see a man seated at a bare writing table behind blocks of stone and bars of steel. In order to consume the burden of time and release nervous energy, he jotted down some of his thoughts. John Bunyan would have been the last to have presumed that what he did at that bare writing table would penetrate beyond those walls and result in one of the three or four most influential books in the history of western Christendom.

In Frauenberg there is a drab two-story house. On the second floor is a small workroom, which in the sixteenth century was the workroom of a monk named Copernicus. In imagination we can see him peering into the heavens at night and jotting down his observations. Copernicus would have scoffed at the suggestion that what he did in that little room would create one of the major scientific revolutions in the history of mankind. Some time later another man used his astronomical telescope to prove that the earth rotated daily upon its axis. Galileo had no reason to believe that he too had penetrated beyond the span of history by proving the Copernican theory.

*From an address by Dr. Dean F. Berkley*

# Lincoln's Modesty

□ Lincoln's ambition was tempered by a pervasive modesty, perhaps the most clearly defined attribute of this style. "If the good people choose to keep me in the background," the young Railsplitter said in his first political communication, "I have been too familiar with disappointment to be much chagrined." When Lincoln looked for a political job after his single term in Congress, Herndon recalled that "melancholy dripped from him as he walked." "There is nothing about me," Lincoln said, "which would authorize me to think of a first class office." Less than a year before his nomination in Chicago, he wrote, "I must say I do not think myself fit for the Presidency." After he had been nominated, he wrote a defeated candidate identifying himself as "the humblest of all whose names were before the convention." In submitting his letter of acceptance to the chairman of the Notification Committee, he hoped his answer was "sufficiently brief to do no harm." After the Republican victories of 1863, he was glad that he had not, "by native depravity . . . done anything bad enough to prevent the good result." After his Gettysburg Address, he told Edward Everett, "I am pleased to know that, in your judgment, the little I did say was not entirely a failure." When the actor, James Hackett, published a personal letter reflecting upon his literary accomplishment, Lincoln assured Hackett he was used to such criticism. "I have endured a great deal of ridicule without much malice; and I have received a great deal of kindness, not quite free from ridicule."

A mystical determinism pervaded Lincoln's thinking and enhanced his sense of humility. "I claim not to have controlled events," he said, "but confess plainly that events have controlled me." *From an address by Robert G. Gunderson*

# Washington's Prayer for America

□ Two centuries have not tarnished the towering image of George Washington, "first in war, first in peace, first in the hearts of his countrymen."

He was the one indispensable man of the Revolution, a man of action among men of prodigious vision. He found the union a dream and left it a reality.

Throughout a life guided by unselfish patriotism, he displayed hallmarks of greatness that were noted by his contemporaries and posterity alike. The profound strength of character that distinguished his every public action, found expression in this simple prayer for the young republic that was destined to become the greatest free power in the history of the world.

Almighty God,

We make our earnest prayer that Thou wilt keep the United States in Thy holy protection;

That Thou wilt incline the hearts of the citizens to cultivate a spirit of subordination and obedience to government;

To entertain a brotherly affection and love for one another and for their fellow citizens at large.

And finally, that Thou will most graciously be pleased to dispose us all to do justice, and love mercy,

159

And to demean ourselves with that charity, humility, and pacific temper of mind which are the characteristics of the Divine Author.

Without an humble imitation of these things we can never hope to become a happy nation.

Grant our supplication, we beseech Thee, through Jesus Christ, our Lord. Amen.

# Paul Revere

□ Patriot's Day, April 19, is officially celebrated in Maine and Massachusetts in commemoration of the Battle of Lexington and Concord. In a sworn statement still preserved, Paul Revere, the most famous patriot of that momentous day, declared that while he did reach Lexington half an hour ahead to William Dawes, who started from Boston two hours ahead of him, he never "came to Concord town," but was captured. Of the three messengers, Samuel Prescott alone rode through. Paul Revere did a lot of riding, bearing dispatches for the colonial authorities, but that was only a trivial incident in his notable career of service to the nation. He was an important manufacturer, and the founder of the copper and brass manufacturing industry in the United States.

# Criticism

□ No one really welcomes criticism. It is a threat to our sense of security. And yet, a mark of our maturity is our ability to take criticism—to listen and to learn from it, even though for a time the process is painful.

This capacity to listen and to learn was demonstrated by Abraham Lincoln. At one period of crisis during the Civil War Lincoln sent an important message to Stanton, his Secretary of War. The messenger returned in obvious embarrassment. "Did you deliver my message?" the President asked. "Yes, I did." "And what did Mr. Stanton say?" The messenger looked down at the floor and hesitated to speak. "Mr. Stanton tore up your letter," the messenger replied at long last in a barely audible whisper, "and he said that you are a fool." "Mr. Stanton called me a fool?" asked the President. "Yes, sir."

There was a moment of silence, then Abraham Lincoln said, "Well, if Mr. Stanton says that I am a fool I must be one. Mr. Stanton is generally right. I had better look into the matter." Now, there is a mature response to criticism. Lincoln was a sensitive man. No doubt that criticism hurt him. And yet, rather than responding in angry self-defense, rather than resenting Stanton's action and rebuking him, rather than barking back—Lincoln mused, "I had better look into the matter."

*From* Praying Hands

# Humility

□ Many people are surprised to learn of the humility of President Lincoln. It is amazing to recount the personal indignities to which Lincoln was willing to subject himself if he thought it would help the Union. General George B. McClellan became the opposition presidential candidate on an anti war program in 1864. As commander in chief of the Army of the Potomac, he was at times almost insolent to his commander in chief, Abraham Lincoln. An outstanding episode was the occasion when Lincoln and two of his officials went to call on General McClellan in the evening. They were told that the general was out to dinner so they said they would wait for his return. When he did return, he went directly to bed, ignoring the fact that the president of the United States was calling on him. Yet Lincoln said nothing and did not remove McClellan from command until, long after, he was convinced that McClellan was no longer the man to head the Union forces.

Some of you also may remember that Secretary of State Seward in an almost insulting memorandum asked Lincoln to surrender the real executive power to him. Seward also issued confusing orders on the expedition to relieve Fort Sumter. Lincoln's answer to this effrontery was a mild and tolerant attitude which later led Seward to respect and finally to love him. Lincoln, through his humility, transformed Seward from an insubordinate party leader to a great secretary of state and a great supporter.

161

Lincoln appointed Stanton, secretary of war, although he knew the latter had called him a "gawky, long-armed ape" when they were lawyers on a case together.

Another episode which must have been hard to stomach was the appointment of Salmon P. Chase as chief justice of the United States. Chase, as a member of Lincoln's cabinet, had actively connived for his own election to the presidency in 1864. He had formed political conspiracies against Lincoln and his policies on several occasions. Yet Lincoln kept Chase in his cabinet for years. When it became clear that it would help keep the radical wing in the Republican party and thus aid the Union to appoint Chase chief justice of the Supreme Court, Lincoln did so without hesitation.                         *From an address by Dr. George C. S. Benson*

# The Beauty Remains

□ The French artist, Pierre Auguste Renoir, suffered a great deal from an old malady, rheumatism. It was particularly painful for him to continue painting, which he did seated in a chair.

One day a friend passed while he was forcing himself to work. Noting Renoir's obvious pain, the friend exclaimed, "You have done enough already, Renoir. Why do you continue to torture yourself?"

The artist looked at him for a long moment and replied, "The pain passes, but the beauty remains."

We all have our moments of pain and our memories of beauty. And it is the beauty in life that sustains us through whatever moments of pain may come.

# A Rush Job

□ It took "O. Henry" (William Sidney Porter) not more than three hours to write his most celebrated story, *The Gift of the Magi*. He had to meet a deadline for the special Sunday Christmas edition of a New York newspaper in December, 1905.

*Sunshine Magazine*

# The Age of Achievement

☐ "Almost everything that is great has been done by youth." That's what one English statesman thought, and the names in the lefthand column below support his theory. But look also at the righthand column. There's proof, too, that no one should have to apologize for being over 30.

—Mozart was 8 when he composed his first symphony.

—Alexander the Great made his major military conquests while he was in his twenties.

—Albert Einstein published his first articles on the theory of relativity when he was 26.

—Jane Addams founded Hull House when she was 29.

Alexander Graham Bell patented the telephone when he was 29.

—Michelangelo completed his famous Pieta by the age of 26.

—Samuel Colt patented his first revolver in his early twenties.

—John Keats wrote most of his best known poems when he was 23.

—Cervantes completed *Don Quixote* when he was nearing 70.

—Clara Barton, at 59, founded the American Red Cross.

—Goethe finished the dramatic poem *Faust* at 82.

—Verdi composed *Otello* at 73, *Falstaff* in his late seventies.

—Leonardo da Vinci painted the Mona Lisa when he was around 50.

—Dostoyevsky wrote his first great novel, *Crime and Punishment,* at 45.

—George Bernard Shaw wrote his famous drama *Saint Joan* at 67.

—Benjamin Disraeli became Prime Minister of England for the second time at 70. He's the one who said, "Almost everything that is great has been done by youth."

* Reprinted by permission from Changing Times, The Kiplinger Magazine *(March 1969 issue). Copyright 1969 by the Kiplinger Washington Editors, Inc., 1729 H Street, N.W., Washington, D.C. 20006*

# Think of Beauty

□ Frank Lloyd Wright, the famous architect, once said to a group of young people: "Think of beauty, think of poetry, remember your spirit, consider your growth. These are the important things. You will be successful if you have the gift to pursue beauty. You will not have to push others out of the way or compromise or steal and lose your ideal. It is not easy to find it once you have lost it—the pressure of life is too strong by then."

# The Eyes Have It

□ The genius Leonardo da Vinci, renowned master painter and inventor, is also famed in the annals of ophthalmology because he was the first to describe the cameralike action of the eye. About 1508 he recorded the earliest theory of contact lenses.

Spectacles weren't introduced until 1300. Before that time, millions of people lived out their lives never being able to see mountains, clouds, or stars.

Benjamin Franklin invented bifocal lenses in 1784.

# Hope

□ In 1801 a very great man by the name of William Wilberforce, whose work in behalf of the black people of the world endears him to posterity, said, "I dare not marry, the future of the world is so unsettled." In 1806 William Pitt, one of the greatest statesmen in history, declared, "There is scarcely anything around us but ruin and despair." In 1848 Lord Shaftesbury, whose work among the poor in England marks him as one of the great humanitarians of all time, said, "Nothing can save the British Empire from shipwreck." How wrong he was is indicated by the fact that the sixty-year reign of Queen Victoria brought the British Empire to the apex of its greatness.

In 1849 Benjamin Disraeli, who later became a chief confidant of Queen Victoria, said: "In industry, commerce, and agriculture there is no hope." And in 1852, on his deathbed, the Duke of Wellington, who apparently was rather glad he was dying, made this statement: "I thank God I shall be spared from seeing the consummation of ruin that is gathering about us in this world."

Well, friends, do these comments strike you as familiar? Haven't you read similar statements in the current press or heard them over radio or television? Ah, yes, there are people who spend their lives insisting that the world is going to pieces. But the world still blunders along, hoping for something better, striving for something nobler. And the world will attain that if it keeps enthusiasm working for it. *Dr. Norman Vincent Peale*

## What Is Home?

□ The late Madame Ernestine Schumann-Heink, who sang her way into the hearts of the world, wrote this description of home:

"A roof to keep out the rain. Four walls to keep out the wind. Floors to keep out the cold. Yes, but home is more than that. It is the laugh of a baby, the song of a mother, the strength of a father. Warmth of loving hearts, light from happy eyes, kindness, loyalty, comradeship.

"Home is the first school, and the first church for young ones, where they learn what is right, what is good, and what is kind. Where they go for comfort when they are hurt or sick. Where joy is shared and sorrow eased. Where fathers and mothers are respected and loved. Where children are wanted. Where the simplest food is good enough for kings because it is earned. Where money is not so important as loving-kindness. Where even the teakettle sings from happiness. That is home. God bless it." *Praying Hands*

## If You Can Keep It

□ As Benjamin Franklin walked out of Convention Hall he was asked: "What have you given us?" And Franklin, past eighty, yet with his great mind still looking to the future, gave his answer to that question: "A republic, sir, if you can keep it."

# Why He Was Good

□ Just before the great Paderewski sailed for Europe after completing a highly successful concert tour of the United States, he made this statement:

"There have been a few moments when I have known complete satisfaction, but only a few. I have rarely been free from the disturbing realization that my playing might have been better."

The secret of Paderewski's greatness lay in his dissatisfaction with his own efforts. As long as he remained unhappy about his playing, he was constantly striving to improve himself. Although the world held him to be perfect, he himself knew his own weaknesses, and kept constantly at the job of improving his technique. *Sunshine Magazine*

# He Did Well

□ Composer Sigmund Romberg's operetta *Desert Song* received a lukewarm reception when it opened on Broadway. Romberg, who had invested his own savings in the venture, was depressed. His wife, however, was more confident. She even offered to buy his share of the show. "Buy it? I'll give it to you gladly," he said.

After a few weeks the show suddenly caught on and became a hit. Romberg's friends were jubilant. "You see how you can never know," they said to him. "Just a few weeks ago, you thought you were a failure. Now you have success and fame." "Yes," said Romberg happily, "and I have a rich wife, too."

*St. Louis Post-Dispatch*

# Music

□ Jenny Lind had a wonderful time touring the East. One day she attended a gala picnic in Springfield, Massachusetts. The slender, beautifully gowned prima donna was asked to favor the joyous throng with a song. Standing in a wild-fern enclosure amid elms, white oaks, maples, only the blue vault of heaven overhead, she began an impromptu recital.

While rapt in song, her listeners commenced to note an unusual fluttering of wings. They flew in from everywhere—robins, blue-birds, orioles, cardinals. As Miss Lind filled the woodlands with mountain airs, the branches were podiums of celestial music; each branch became a rainbow of colors and the rainbow sang. Trembling, voiceless, she stood silent and threw a kiss, and another. The prima donna's face was wet with tears. She wept in sheer rapture.

*Reverend Philip Jerome Cleveland,*
Church Management

# From Actor to Inventor

□ The advent of the sewing machine might have been indefinitely delayed if Isaac Meritt Singer had been sucessful as a Shakesperean actor.

Born in Pittston, New York, in 1811, Singer ran away from home at the age of 12 and went to work as an apprentice machinist in Rochester. He soon became a qualified journeyman, but fell in love with the stage and for 20 years he persisted in his attempts to reach theatrical stardom although he hardly, if ever, managed to advance above the role of bit-player.

Finally in the early 1840's, when his touring company was stranded in Fredericksburg, Ohio, he was forced to seek work in a woodworking plant. He invented a carving machine and scraped up enough money to go east and start a business. In New York he teamed up with a printer named Goerge Zieber and they moved to Boston where they rented space to display the carving machine in the workroom of Orson C. Phelps, a struggling sewing machine manufacturer.

Although the first sewing machine patent had gone to Elias Howe, Jr., the latter had failed to launch his product successfully in America and a number of machines of a similar type were produced by others. One of these was the Phelps machine which had been built by John A. Leroy and S. C. Blodgett. The machine had many faults, however, and a high breakdown rate.

Singer was certain he could correct all the "bugs" and he did just that. He replaced the circular shuttle that twisted the thread with a horizontal one; designed a table to support the cloth, a presser-foot to hold the cloth down at the upward stroke of the needle, and replaced the cumbersome hand crank with a foot pedal.

The altered machine proved an immediate success and within a few years the company was doing a land-office business, going on to develop into one of the greatest enterprises in industrial history.

*Sunshine Magazine*


# The Homeless

□ "I was born with music in my system," said Fritz Kreisler, the great violinist. "I knew musical scores instinctively before I knew my ABC's. It was a gift of Providence. I did not acquire it. So I do not deserve thanks for the music. Music is too sacred to be sold. I never look upon the money I earn as my own. It is public money. It is only a fund entrusted to my care for proper disbursement. . . . In all these years of my so-called success in music, we have not built a home for ourselves. Between it and us stand all the homeless in the world."

*Reverend A. P. Bailey,* Chicago Tribune


# Young in Heart

□ Recently I realized, much to my surprise, for I have been doing it unconsciously, that every night just before I go to sleep I repeat the same little prayer of my childhood, with my same childhood faith and trust. Me, a grown-up woman, a Hollywood actress, a mother, a wife, saying just before I close my eyes, "And please, dear God, make me a good girl."

Momentarily I was upset. One reads so much of complexes these days that simplicity is regarded as suspect. Could I be trying, subconsciously, to escape the responsibility for carrying an adult burden in an adult world? So I checked with my mother.

"Mother," I asked, "is there any special prayer that you say every night before you go to sleep?"

My mother, a wise servant of God, serving Him so faithfully and well for so many years, thought a minute and then said, "Yes, there is. I say, 'Give me a happy death and please, dear God, make me a good girl.' "

In the simplicity of that prayer, in that childlike attitude of the heart, lie, I am convinced, some of our biggest answers.

*Loretta Young, actress,* Praying Hands

# He Didn't Know

□ Franz Liszt, a pianist who was a favorite of royalty, received decorations galore from the crowned heads of Europe.

One night at a reception, he was seated next to a general whose chest was also adorned with medals and ribbons. The general eyed Liszt's decorations and said with a sneer: "I didn't know you were in battle."

Replied Liszt: "And I didn't know you played the piano."

# Getting Along with Others

□ Not so many years ago, there was a man who lived his declining years on a small pension, practically alone, and spent much of his time feeding pigeons. Yet, he might well have lived those years in affluence, among friends who respected him, but—he could not get along with people.

Nikola Tesla came to this country from Austro-Hungary in the late 1880's and was a contemporary of Thomas Edison and George Westinghouse. Inventor of the induction motor, he contributed many improvements in the practical uses of electricity.

But with his brains and ability, Tesla also brought with him from the old country a habit of walking out on jobs when he thought someone hurt his feelings. In many instances, his grievances might well have been adjusted satisfactorily, if Tesla had been less haughty and not so quick to walk out.

One incident particularly reveals this personality fault. He and Edison were jointly offered the Nobel Prize for physics in 1912. Tesla refused to share the prize on the grounds that Edison was not his equal in scientific discoveries. The prize eventually went to a third person.

During his creative years, Tesla, of course, could find other employment; but the time came when he was no longer creative enough to do that. Then when the friends he might have made, and the substance he might have accumulated, were needed, he did not have them. *Sunshine Magazine*

# A Song in His Heart

□ Some years ago a Catholic friend of mine, whom I call affectionately "Father Bob," told me the following story. A wealthy business man, visiting a leper colony, watched a Sister of Mercy change the dressings on a desperately ill patient. "Sister," said the visitor, obviously shaken, "I would not do what you are doing for a million dollars!" "No," replied the girl with a smile, "Neither would I."

I have just finished reading the life of Robert Louis Stevenson, my favorite author of adventure tales and stirring verse. No one who is familiar with his courageous and cheerful battle against tuberculosis can fail to be moved by his gay writings, his vivid imagination, his astonishing joie de vivre.

When Stevenson visited the leper colony at Molokai, Hawaii, he was greatly touched by the tragedy of this terrible and, at that time, incurable disease. In order to cheer the younger patients, he taught them croquet. The good Sisters, grateful for his kindness, nevertheless warned him to wear gloves when he handled the mallets. This Stevenson refused to do, lest he offend the children who treated him as one of themselves.

Space does not permit recording further incidents in the life of this great man, but to those who knew him, he showed a truly Christian attitude in his love for his fellowman, his kindness towards animals, his sterling honesty and generosity, and always, no matter how ill, a zest for life that nothing could quench.

Under the wide and starry sky,
Dig the grave and let me lie;
Glad did I live and gladly die,
And I laid me down with a will.

This be the verse you grave for me.
Here he lies where he longed to be;
Home is the sailor, home from sea,
And the hunter home from the hill.
                    *James L. Jenks, Jr.*, Praying Hands


# Stupid

☐ Out in our part of the country we think a great deal about football. But, you know, there's a game that we always watch, and I am sure that many of you watch it, too. It's when the great battle takes place between Oklahoma and Texas.

Coach Darrell Royal tells this story about one of those great battles, when Oklahoma had Texas down on their own two yard line and Coach Royal, being under pressure, decided that he was going to call the quarterback over and tell him exactly what to do.

So, he called the quarterback over, and he said, "Listen, when you get back out there, first I want you to get hold of that ball and I want you to really hold onto the ball.

"And then second, I want you to have another quarterback sneak. I want you to hold onto that ball.

"Now third, now get this, third I want you to punt. Now let's review it. I want you to do it exactly the way I tell you. What do you do first?"

"Quarterback sneak."

"That's right!"

"What do you do second?"

"Quarterback sneak."

"That's right! What do you do third?"

"Punt."

He said, "You've got it! Now, son, I want you to get out there and play as you've never played before."

171

This old quarterback went running out, kicking up the astro turf. They had their first quarterback sneak. He held onto that ball, and he went clear down to the middle of the field.

There, in the middle of the field, he lined those men up again. He had that second quarterback sneak, and he went clear down to the Oklahoma two yard line.

There, on the Oklahoma two yard line, he lined those people up again, and he punted.

Coach Royal called him over and he said, "My heavens, man, what were you thinking about—punting on the two yard line?"

He said, "I was thinking what a stupid coach to have me punt on the two yard line!"
*Donald O. Clifton*

## Not Until Then

□ "I will tell you sir, what I think of your poetical works; they will be read when Shakespeare's and Milton's are forgotten"—then after a pause—"but not until then."
*Richard Porson to Robert Southey*

## Queen Victoria and Lewis Carroll

□ Queen Victoria was very much impressed by *Alice in Wonderland* and commanded her secretary to write and compliment the author, the Reverend C. L. Dodgson (Lewis Carroll) adding that she would be pleased to receive any other book by him. He sent her a copy of his *Syllabus of Plane Algebraical Geometry*.
*Leslie Missen*

## A Good Title

□ In 1938 Mr. Churchill published an English edition of his speeches called *Arms and the Covenant*. At that time the American public took little interest either in arms or in the League of

172

Nations. Mr. Churchill was therefore asked to suggest another title for the American edition.

Willing to oblige, Mr. Churchill telegraphed back "The Years of the Locust." The telegram was mutilated in transmission and arrived as "The Years of the Lotus." The American publishers were nonplussed. At last one of them had a flash of inspiration. The lotus induces sleep and from this premise he produced the title *While England Slept*. Mr. Churchill agreed at once, and the American edition went through the states like wildfire.    *London Times*

# Courage

□ When Western Union offered to buy the ticker invented by Thomas Edison, the great inventor was unable to name a price. Edison asked for a couple of days to consider it. Talking the matter over with his wife, she suggested he ask $20,000, but this seemed exorbitant to Edison. At the appointed time, Edison returned to the Western Union office. He was asked to name his price. "How much?" asked the Western Union official. Edison tried to say $20,000, but lacked the courage, and just stood there speechless.

The official waited a moment, then broke the silence and said, "Well, how about $100,000?"

# Facing It

□ A tramp, when asked about his philosophy of life, replied, "I turn my back to the wind." That probably is why he was a tramp. Following the line of least resistance is what makes rivers and many men crooked. A man cannot drift to success.

In contrast to this philosophy is the statement which Captain MacWhite spoke to his mate in Joseph Conrad's immortal tale of the sea, *Typhoon*. In the midst of a great storm, MacWhite said: "Keep facing it! They may say what they like—the heaviest seas run with the wind. Always facing it! That's the way to get through!"

# Character

□ King George of England once sought a governess for his children. Impressed with what he heard of a certain Scottish lady, he offered the position to her. She declined, saying she had not enough learning to instruct such children.

The king, however, insisted, "Madam, I want a right-minded person to take charge of my children. I can easily buy accomplishments, but I cannot buy character."

# He Didn't Lose

□ President Cleveland, while talking to a friend about one of his many angling expeditions, told the following story: "It is remarkable," said the president, "how mean some people are. I had with me on that particular trip two countrymen who evidently were familiar with my reputation as an angler. Before starting, one of them made the following suggestion: 'Mr. President,' said he, 'we will agree that the first one who catches a fish must treat the crowd.'

"I assented, and we started. Now those two fellows both had bites and were too mean to pull them up."

"I suppose you lost, then," remarked the friend.

"Oh, no!" replied the president. "I didn't have any bait on my hook."

# The Perils of Wrong Judgment

□ The victorious Duke of Wellington, after his retirement, used to invite the officers who served with him in the Battle of Waterloo to a yearly banquet, where they discussed the exciting experiences of other days.

At one of these annual events, the Duke produced a lovely jewel box, small, but encrusted with diamonds. The box was passed around the table for the guests to admire.

After some time the duke asked for the return of the jewel box.

His guests were startled, as no one remembered who held it last. A careful search of the table and floor revealed nothing. At this stage in the proceedings someone suggested that all the guests present submit to being searched. Two raised objections to this proposal— one, a guest, who declared he had not taken the jewel box but who would not agree to be searched; the other, the Duke himself, who flatly refused to have his former officers suffer this indignity.

The banquet ended with the box still missing. The guests departed, including the one who had refused to be searched (and consequently was regarded with suspicion). Some days later the Duke found his jewel box in an inside pocket of his coat! It had been returned to him the night of the banquet, and while engaged in conversation, he had picked up the box without thinking and slipped it in his inside pocket.

At once the Duke set out to find the guest who had declined to be searched. He found the officer living in a poor section of the city nursing his sick wife. After informing him that the missing box had been found, the Duke inquired, "Why did you object to being searched, thus drawing suspicion upon you?"

The officer replied, "In my pocket that night was a large part of my meal, slipped from the plate into a paper bag, that I might take food to my wife."

How often, when we criticize unfavorably, we do not know all the circumstances!

*William J. Thompson, "Rays of Sunshine," in* Praying Hands

# Life Has Never Lost

□ A quarter of a century ago at Colombey the late Charles de Gaulle wrote the following words which express something of his greatness in solitude. "Yet, on our little property—I have walked around it fifteen thousand times—the trees, stripped by the cold, rarely fail to turn green again, and the flowers my wife has planted bloom once more each spring. The village houses are decrepit, but suddenly laughing girls and boys come out of their doors.

"When I walk to one of the nearby woods . . . their solemn depths fill me with nostalgia. But suddenly the song of a bird, the sun through the leaves, or the buds of a thicket remind me that ever since it has existed on earth, life wages a battle it has never lost. Then I feel a secret solace passing through me. Since everything eternally begins anew, what I have done will sooner or later be a source of new ardor after I have gone."

Then a little later he adds that love raises "certitudes so radiant and powerful they will never end."

*As quoted in*
The Christian Science Monitor

# Have Hope

☐ Louis Pasteur never studied science until he was in his twenties.

Hans Christian Anderson was a nearly starved ham actor but at age thirty wrote his *Fairy Tales*.

Harry Truman was turned down by West Point and became a haberdashery salesman.

Thomas Edison's grade school teacher wrote his mother that he should be switched to remedial school as he was inattentive and indolent.

# New Experiences

A Story About Wm. McC. Martin, Former Chairman
of the Federal Reserve Board and
of the New York Stock Exchange

☐ When I was first invited to take on this assignment, I was asked to "just tell them what monetary policy is all about." More than thirty years ago, when I worked at the Federal Reserve Bank of Richmond, I could have done this with rather more self-assurance than I feel tonight.

In taking a "tell it like it is" approach, I am reminded of one of former Chairman Martin's stories about himself. It seems that when he was at the New York Stock Exchange back in the 1940s he exercised regularly at a well-known nearby gymnasium run by a man named "Gunboat" Smith. One day "Gunboat" was bemoaning the fact that one of his preliminary fighters in a charity fight that evening at Madison Square Garden had had to drop out and he asked Mr. Martin if he would substitute. The Chairman thought about it awhile and, as he puts it, decided that "after all, life was just a series of experiences." So he accepted the engagement. It seems, however, that word got around the street and that night a crowd from the Exchange showed up at the fight. Mr. Martin relates that he managed to get through three rounds, although when he looked over at the other man and saw him glowering, all he could do was smile back because he wasn't mad at anyone! At any rate, at the end of the fight the referee lifted Mr. Martin's arm, too, called it a draw, and the men from the Exchange climbed into the ring and carried our former chairman off on their shoulders.

This story typifies not only Mr. Martin's attitude toward life but illustrates why he was so well suited to manage monetary policy. His ability to treat each experience as it came along stood him in good stead.

*J. Dewey Daane, Member, Board of Governors*
*of the Federal Reserve System*

# Benjamin Franklin

□ Benjamin Franklin made many contributions to human thought and left useful inventions to make life easier.

History has remembered his witty sayings, but his practical contributions are sometimes overlooked.

On May 23, 1775, Franklin invented bifocal glasses. The wearer could use the same glasses for ordinary vision and for reading. Those practical bifocals were an expression of Franklin's concern for the commonplace.

Franklin's philosophy might also be considered as bifocal—he had a clear and sharply defined image of the near as well as the far. His creed is well established in this epitaph written by himself.

> The body of
> Benjamin Franklin, printer,
> (Like the cover of an old book,
> Its contents worn out,

And stript of its lettering
and gilding)
Lies here, food for worms!
Yet the work itself shall
not be lost,
For it will, as he believed,
appear once more
In a new
And more beautiful edition,
Corrected and amended
By its Author!

*Praying Hands*

# Leaving His Possessions

□ A brilliant Polish scientist suffering from muscular dystrophy, was asked how he managed to go on cheerfully and with such faith. He said, "When I escaped from Poland I had to leave all my worldly possessions, and found I could survive. When I take leave of this life, again I shall be leaving all my possessions, including this body. What does it matter that I begin now to live more in the spirit than the flesh? It will not be long before that will be my only habitat, and I find it sufficient and creative beyond belief!"

*Praying Hands*

# Paying Others

□ Thomas Dreier tells the story of a man over eighty who was observed by a neighbor planting a small peach tree.

"Do you expect to eat peaches from that tree?" the neighbor said.

The old gentleman rested on his spade. "No," he said. "At my age I know I won't. But all my life I've enjoyed peaches—never from a tree I had planted myself. I wouldn't have had peaches if other men hadn't done what I'm doing now. I'm just trying to pay the other fellows who planted peach trees for me."

178

In practicing giving-away we both plant peach trees and eat peaches, often unconscious of the fruits of our own little unthoughtfulnesses and equally of the thoughtfulnesses others have invested for our benefit, perhaps many years ago.

Today's giving-away is a blind investment in future happiness, though we can never tell when, where, or in what form this happiness will come.

Which is part of the fun! *Praying Hands*

# Courtesy

□ Before William McKinley became the twenty-fifth president of the United States, he served in Congress. Going to his office one day he boarded a streetcar, and took the only seat available. Moments later a woman who appeared to be ill also boarded the car, stood in front of a fellow congressman, who hid behind the newspaper he was reading and did not offer her a seat. McKinley walked up the aisle, tapped the woman on the shoulder, offered her his seat, and took her place clutching a strap.

Years later, when McKinley was president, this same congressman was recommended for the post of an ambassador to a foreign country. McKinley refused to appoint him, fearing that if the man hadn't had the common courtesy to offer his seat in a crowded streetcar, he would also lack the courtesies inherent in a man soon to become a great ambassador to a troubled nation. The disappointed congressman bemoaned his fate to all friends who would listen, but could never figure out why he had been refused.

*Praying Hands*

# The Bible

□ A noted orator asked Dickens for the most pathetic story in literature, and he said it was that of the prodigal son. Mr. Coleridge was asked for the richest passage in literature, and he said it was the first sixteen verses of the fifth chapter of Matthew. Another asked Daniel Webster for the greatest legal digest, and he

179

replied that it was the Sermon on the Mount. No one has equaled David for poetry, nor Isaiah for vision, nor Jesus for His moral and ethical teachings, nor Peter for holy zeal, nor Apollos for fiery oratory, nor Paul for logic, nor John's statement of sanctified love. God's Word is the very greatest of all the books, and its Author the very greatest of all teachers. We do well to stay close to its pages. It is *the* Book. *The Lutheran Digest*

# He Gave His Best

□ Someone once asked Al Jolson, popular musical comedy star of the twenties, what he did when he ran into a cold audience. Al Jolson said: "Whenever I go out before an audience and don't get the response I feel that I ought to get, what do I do. I don't go back behind the scenes and say to myself, 'That audience is dead from the neck up—it's a bunch of wooden nutmegs.' No, instead I say to myself, 'Look here, Al, what is wrong with you tonight. The audience is all right, but you're all wrong, Al.' "

Instead of giving up and putting on a poor show with the excuse that the audience couldn't appreciate a good one, Al tried to give the best performance of his career . . . he had them applauding and begging for more. Nuggets, *Barnes-Ross Co.*

# Battles or Babies

□ One hundred and sixty years ago men were following with bated breath the march of Napoleon, and waiting with feverish impatience for news of the wars. And all the while, in their own homes, babies were being born.

But who could think about babies? Everyone was thinking about battles.

In one year, midway between Trafalgar and Waterloo, there stole into the world a host of heroes. Gladstone was born in Liverpool, Tennyson at the Somersby Rectory, and Oliver Wendell Holmes in Massachusetts; and the very same day of that same year, Charles Darwin made his debut at Shrewsbury, and Abraham

Lincoln drew his first breath in old Kentucky. Music was enriched by the advent of Felix Mendelssohn at Hamburg.

But nobody thought of babies; everyone was thinking of battles. Yet which of the battles of 1809 mattered more than the babies of 1809? *Sunshine Magazine*

# The Fisherman's Prayer

☐ Herbert Hoover was an ardent lover of outdoor sports, especially fishing. Once when a friend questioned him about the future life, he quoted the "Fisherman's Prayer":

"God, grant that I may fish until my dying day! And when it comes to my last cast, I humbly pray: When in God's landing net I'm peacefully asleep, that in His mercy I may be judged as good enough to keep." *Praying Hands*

# Greediness

☐ Mr. Noland Diller, who was one of Mr. Lincoln's neighbors in Springfield, tells the following:

I was called to the door one day by the cries of children in the street, and there was Mr. Lincoln, striding by with two of his boys, both of whom were wailing aloud. "Why, Mr. Lincoln, what's the matter with the boys?" I asked.

"Just what's the matter with the whole world," Lincoln replied. "I've got three walnuts, and each wants two."

# I Shall Go There!

☐ Many interesting anecdotes have been recorded about Joseph Conrad, one of the truly great novelists of the world. One of the most inspiring is to the effect that when he was a child of ten he was fascinated by a book of adventures in the Congo region of Africa. Putting his little finger on the pink spot which represented

181

Congo on the map, he declared to his playmates, "Someday I shall go there!"

And though a penniless Polish lad, and the spot he indicated was five thousand miles away, he did eventually visit and explore the mysterious land which had so captivated his childish fancy.

Yet that adventure was only an incident in the amazing life-journey of Joseph Conrad—from cabin boy on the rough sailing vessels of 75 years ago, speaking only a few words of broken English, to the foremost novelist of the day, acknowledged master of English prose.

He went where he wanted to go. And as generally happens when a man shows that he knows where he is going, the world stood aside to let him pass. Sunshine Magazine

# Ether

□ Dr. Oliver Wendell Holmes, father of the jurist, handed down some momentous decisions himself. One was rendered during the time when the entire populace of Boston was embroiled in a bitter quarrel trying to determine to which of their native sons belonged the credit for the discovery of ether. One faction hotly contended that credit should go to Dr. W. T. G. Morton, and the other supported Dr. Charles T. Jackson just as vigorously.

"May I suggest," said Dr. Holmes, "that we have built on a single base, statues of both these men and inscribe the monument: 'To Ether.'"

# Part Five

---

## PERTINENT
## QUOTATIONS
## FROM LITERATURE

# Ability

□ In the last analysis ability is commonly found to consist mainly in a high degree of solemnity.  *Ambrose Bierce*

\* \* \*

□ 'Tis God gives skill,
But not without men's hands: He
could not make
Antonio Stradivari's violins
Without Antonio.

*George Eliot*

# Acquisitiveness

□ My wants are many, and, if told,
Would muster many a score;
And were each wish a mine of gold,
I still should long for more.

*John Quincy Adams*

# Action

□ One hour of life, crowded to the full with glorious action, and filled with noble risks, is worth whole years of those mean observances of paltry decorum.  *Sir Walter Scott*

# Adversity

☐ Sweet are the uses of adversity,
Which, like the toad, ugly and venomous,
Wears yet a precious jewel in his head.

*William Shakespeare*

* * *

☐ Never give up! if adversity presses,
Providence wisely has mingled the cup,
And the best counsel, in all your distresses,
Is the stout watchword of "never give up!"

*Martin Farquhar Tupper*

# Advice

☐ In June the air is full of advice. People are graduating and getting married and setting out on vacations, and it is the fate of these people to be battered with advice until they scream for mercy.                                             *Russell Baker*

# Age

☐ Youth is perennially, and naturally, in revolt against age. Only by belittling the past can one assure himself and the world of his importance. Nobody, at 20, is going to admit the possibility that all the best poems may have been written, the best pictures painted, the best music composed.                     *Bruce Bliven*

* * *

☐ In youth we clothe ourselves with rainbows, and go as brave as the zodiac. In age, we put out another sort of perspiration,—gout, fever, rheumatism, caprice, doubt, fretting, avarice.

*Ralph Waldo Emerson*

◻ Youth is the time for the adventures of the body, but age for the triumphs of the mind.                    *Logan Pearsall Smith*

\* \* \*

◻ If we could be twice young and twice old we could correct all our mistakes.                    *Euripides*

# Ambition

◻ Every eel hopes to become a whale.                    *German Proverb*

\* \* \*

◻ The ambitious climbs up high and perilous stairs, and never cares how to come down: the desire of rising hath swallowed up his fear of a fall.                    *Thomas Adams*

\* \* \*

◻ In men of the highest character and noblest genius there is to be found an insatiable desire for honor, command, power, and glory.
                    *Cicero*

\* \* \*

◻ What madness is ambition!
What is there in that little breath of men,
Which they call Fame, that should induce the brave
To forfeit ease and that domestic bliss
Which is the lot of happy ignorance?
                    *Philip Freneau*

\* \* \*

◻ Can one desire too much of a good thing?
                    *William Shakespeare*

Ambition is but avarice on stilts and masked.

*Walter Savage Landor*

# Anger

☐ To be wroth with one we love
Doth work like madness in the brain.

*Samuel Taylor Coleridge*

# Aspiration

☐ The statue in the public square is less a portrait of a mortal
individual than a symbol of the immortal aspiration of humanity.

*Mary Antin*

\* \* \*

☐ Ah, but a man's reach should exceed his grasp,
Or what's a Heaven for?

*Robert Browning*

\* \* \*

☐ If you aspire to the highest place it is no disgrace to stop at the
second, or even the third.          *Cicero*

\* \* \*

☐ God, give me hills to climb,
And strength for climbing!

*Arthur Guiterman*

\* \* \*

☐ Heaven is not reached at a single bound;
But we build the ladder by which we rise
From the lowly earth to the vaulted skies,
And we mount to its summit round by round.

*Josiah Gilbert Holland*

□ Build thee more stately mansions, O my soul,
As the swift seasons roll!
Leave thy low-vaulted past!
Let each new temple, nobler than the last,
Shut thee from heaven with a dome more vast,
Till thou at length art free,
Leaving thine outgrown shell by life's unresting sea!

*Oliver Wendell Holmes*

* * *

□ To love the beautiful, to desire the good and to do the best.

*Moses Mendelssohn*

* * *

□ To be what we are, and to become what we are capable of becoming, is the only end of life.     *Robert Louis Stevenson*

* * *

□ I hold it truth, with him who sings
To one clear harp in divers tones,
That men may rise on stepping stones
Of their dead selves to higher things.

*Lord Alfred Tennyson*

# Books

□ Books are the legacies that a great genius leaves in mankind, which are delivered down from generation to generation, as presents to the posterity of those who are yet unborn.

*Joseph Addison*

* * *

□ I would define a book as a work of magic whence escape all kinds of images to trouble the souls and anger the hearts of men.

*Anatole France*

◻ Some books are to be tasted, others to be swallowed, and some few to be chewed and digested.  *Francis Bacon*

\* \* \*

◻ That is a good book which is opened with expectation and closed with profit.  *Amos Bronson Alcott*

\* \* \*

◻ In the best books, great men talk to us, give us their most precious thoughts, and pour their souls into ours.
*William Ellery Channing*

\* \* \*

◻ Books are the quietest and most constant of friends; they are the most accessible and wisest of counsellors, and the most patient of teachers.  *Charles W. Eliot*

\* \* \*

◻ Books and ideas are the most effective weapons against intolerance and ignorance.  *Lyndon B. Johnson*
(This comment was made on Feb. 11, 1964, as he signed into law a bill providing increased federal aid for library services.)

\* \* \*

◻ For books are more than books, they are the life,
The very heart and core of ages past,
The reason why men lived and worked and died,
The essence and quintessence of their lives.
*Amy Lowell*

\* \* \*

◻ The books which help you most are those which make you think the most.  *Theodore Parker*

190

# Chance

□ We do not what we ought,
What we ought not, we do,
And lean upon the thought
That Chance will bring us through.

*Matthew Arnold*

# Character

□ Character is that which reveals moral purpose, exposing the class of things a man chooses or avoids.     *Aristotle*

\* \* \*

□ Talent is nurtured aye in solitude
But Character 'mid the tempests of the world.

*Johann Wolfgang Goethe*

\* \* \*

□ The Porcupine, whom one must Handle, gloved,
May be respected, but is never Loved.

*Arthur Guiterman*

\* \* \*

□ The wisest man could ask no more of Fate
Than to be simple, modest, manly, true,
Safe from the Many, honored by the Few;
To count as naught in World, or Church, or State,
But inwardly in secret to be great.

*James Russell Lowell*

# Circumstances

□ Man is not the creature of circumstances. Circumstances are the creatures of men.     *Benjamin Disraeli*

# Common Sense

□ Common sense is not so common.             *Voltaire*

# Compensation

□ Night brings out stars as sorrow shows us truths.
                                        *Philip James Bailey*

# Conceit

□ Aesop's Fly, sitting on the axle of the chariot, has been much laughed at for exclaiming: What a dust I do raise!
                                        *Thomas Carlyle*

* * *

□ He was like a cock who thought the sun had risen to hear him crow.                                        *George Eliot*

# Confidence

□ They can conquer who believe they can.      *John Dryden*

# Conscience

□ That fierce thing
   They call a conscience.           *Thomas Hood*

* * *

□ There is no witness so terrible, no accuser so potent, as the conscience that dwells in every man's breast.      *Polybius*

# Consistency

☐ Inconsistency is the only thing in which men are consistent.
*Horatio Smith*

# Contemplation

☐ Give me, kind Heaven, a private station,
A mind serene for contemplation.    *John Gay*

# Contentment

☐ The noblest mind the best contentment has.    *Edmund Spenser*

\* \* \*

☐ There are two kinds of discontent in this world: the discontent that works, and the discontent that wrings its hands. The first gets what it wants, and the second loses what it had. There is no cure for the first but success, and there is no cure at all for the second.
*Elbert Hubbard*

# Cosmopolitanism

☐ I am a citizen of the world.    *Diogenes Laertius*

# Courage

☐ Nothing is too high for the daring of mortals; we storm Heaven itself in our folly.    *Horace*

\* \* \*

☐ Last, but by no means least, courage—moral courage, the courage of one's convictions, the courage to see things through. The world is in a constant conspiracy against the brave. It's the age-old struggle—the roar of the crowd on one side and the voice of your conscience on the other.                    *General Douglas MacArthur*

\* \* \*

◻ Give me the serenity to accept what cannot be changed.
Give me the courage to change what can be changed.
The wisdom to know one from the other.
                                        *Reinhold Neibuhr*

\* \* \*

◻ We have hard work to do, and loads to lift;
Shun not the struggle—face it; 'tis God's gift.
                                        *Maltbie Babcock*

\* \* \*

◻ Once to every man and nation comes the moment to decide,
In the strife of Truth with Falsehood, for the good and evil side;
Some great cause, God's new Messiah, offering each the bloom or blight,
Parts the goats upon the left hand, and the sheep upon the right,
And the choice goes by forever 'twixt that darkness and that light.                    *James Russell Lowell*

# Deeds

◻ While you do that which no other man can do, every man is a willing spectator.                    *Ralph Waldo Emerson*

\* \* \*

◻ Well done is better than well said.          *Benjamin Franklin*

194

▢ I count this thing to be grandly true:
That a noble deed is a step toward God.

*Josiah G. Holland*

\* \* \*

▢ The reward for a good deed is to have done it.   *Elbert Hubbard*

\* \* \*

▢ Deeds are better things than words are,
Actions mightier than boastings.

*Henry Wadsworth Longfellow*

\* \* \*

▢ A slender acquaintance with the world must convince every man that actions, not words, are the true criterion.

*George Washington*

# Destiny

▢ There is a divinity that shapes our ends,
Rough-hew them how we will.   *William Shakespeare*

\* \* \*

▢ The tissue of the Life to be
We weave with colors all our own,
And in the field of Destiny
We reap as we have sown.   *John Greenleaf Whittier*

# Disappointment

▢ We mount to heaven mostly on the ruins of our cherished schemes, finding our failures were successes.

*Amos Bronson Alcott*

# Dreams

□ If there were dreams to sell,
What would you buy?

*Thomas Lovell Beddoes*

\* \* \*

□ The republic is a dream.
Nothing happens unless first a dream.

*Carl Sandburg*

\* \* \*

□ All men of action are dreamers.

*James G. Huneker*

\* \* \*

□ Those who dream by night in the dusty recesses of their minds,
wake in the day to find that it was vanity: but the dreamers of the
day are dangerous men, for they may act their dreams with open
eyes, to make it possible.     *Lawrence of Arabia*

# Duty

□ So nigh is grandeur to our dust,
So near is God to man.
When Duty whispers low, Thou must,
The youth replies, I can.

*Ralph Waldo Emerson*

\* \* \*

□ Duty then is the sublimest word in our language. Do your duty
in all things. You cannot do more. You should never wish to do
less.     *Robert E. Lee*

# Education

□ "I only took the regular course," said the Mock Turtle. "Reeling and writhing, of course, to begin with, and then the different branches of Arithmetic—Ambition, Distraction, Uglification and Derision." *Lewis Carroll*

\* \* \*

□ Examinations are formidable even to the best prepared, for the greatest fool may ask more than the wisest man can answer. *Charles Caleb Colton*

\* \* \*

□ 'Tis education forms the common mind:
Just as the twig is bent the tree's inclined. *Alexander Pope*

\* \* \*

□ The whining schoolboy, with his satchel
And shining morning face, creeping like snail
Unwillingly to school. *William Shakespeare*

\* \* \*

□ Education is a thing of which only the few are capable; teach as you will only a small percentage will profit by your most zealous energy. *George Gissing*

\* \* \*

□ School-days, school-days, dear old golden rule days,
Readin' and 'ritin' and 'rithmetic,
Taught to the tune of a hick'ry stick;
You were my queen in calico,
I was your bashful barefoot beau,
And you wrote on my slate, I love you, Joe,
When we were a couple of kids.
*Will D. Cobb,* "School Days"
*(song, 1907, with music by Gus Edwards.)*

197

▢ The only thing more expensive than education is ignorance.

*Herbert V. Prochnow*

\* \* \*

▢ Education makes a people easy to lead, but difficult to drive; easy to govern, but impossible to enslave.

*Baron Brougham and Vaux*

\* \* \*

▢ What greater or better gift can we offer the republic than to teach and instruct our youth? *Cicero*

\* \* \*

▢ The foundation of every state is the education of its youth.

*Diogenes Laertius*

\* \* \*

▢ A learned blockhead is a greater blockhead than an ignorant one. *Benjamin Franklin*

\* \* \*

▢ Education has for its object the formation of Character.

*Herbert Spencer*

\* \* \*

▢ The nation that has the schools has the future.

*Otto Von Bismarck*

\* \* \*

▢ That there should one man die ignorant who had capacity for knowledge, this I call tragedy. *Thomas Carlyle*

◻ Most Americans do value education as a business asset, but not as the entrance into the joy of intellectual experience or acquaintance with the best that has been said and done in the past. They value it not as an experience, but as a tool.     *W. H. P. Faunce*

\* \* \*

◻ Enlighten the people generally and tyranny and oppressions of both mind and body will vanish like evil spirits at the dawn of day.
*Thomas Jefferson*

\* \* \*

◻ At the desk where I sit, I have learned one great truth. The answer for all our national problems—the answer for all the problems of the world—comes down to one single word. That word is *education*.

*Lyndon B. Johnson,*
*Address before the 100th anniversary convocation,*
*Brown University, Providence, R.I.,*
*September 28, 1964*

\* \* \*

◻ Self-education is fine when the pupil is a born educator.
*John A. Shedd*

\* \* \*

◻ A highbrow is a person educated beyond his intelligence.
*Brander Matthews*

\* \* \*

◻ But it was in making education not only common to all, but in some sense compulsory on all, that the destiny of the free republics of America was practically settled.

*James Russell Lowell*

The three Rs of our school system must be supported by the three Ts—teachers who are superior, techniques of instruction that are modern, and thinking about education which places it first in all our plans and hopes.

*Lyndon B. Johnson,*
*Message to Congress, January 12, 1965*

# Egotism

Every bird loves to hear himself sing. *German Proverb*

* * *

The world does not end with the life of any man.
*Winston Churchill*

We are interested in others when they are interested in us.
*Publilius Syrys*

* * *

All the courses of my life do show I am not in the roll of common men. *William Shakespeare*

* * *

Self-love is the greatest of all flatters. *Voltaire*

* * *

To love oneself is the beginning of a life-long romance.
*Oscar Wilde*

# Eloquence

He is an eloquent man who can treat humble subjects with

delicacy, lofty things impressively, and moderate things temperately. *Cicero*

* * *

□ Eloquence is the child of knowledge. *Benjamin Disraeli*

* * *

□ It is the heart which makes man eloquent. *Quintilian*

□ Whatever we conceive well we express clearly, and words flow with ease. *Nicolas Boileau*

# Enemy

□ Our enemies come nearer the truth in the judgments they form of us, than we do in our judgment of ourselves.
*Francois de La Rochefoucauld*

* * *

□ A man's greatness can be measured by his enemy. *Donn Piatt*

# Enthusiasm

□ Every production of genius must be the production of enthusiasm. *Isaac d'Israeli*

* * *

□ Earnestness is enthusiasm tempered by reason. *Blaise Pascal*

* * *

□ Every great and commanding moment in the annals of the world is the triumph of some enthusiasm. *Ralph Waldo Emerson*

201

# Equality

□ Before God we are all equally wise—equally foolish.
*Albert Einstein*

# Error

□ Who errs and mends, to God himself commends.
*Miguel de Cervantes Saavedra*

* * *

□ The man who makes no mistakes does not usually make anything.
*Bishop W. C. Magee*

# Exaggeration

□ We exaggerate misfortune and happiness alike. We are never either so wretched or so happy as we say we are.
*Honore De Balzac*

# Example

□ You can preach a better sermon with your life than with your lips.
*Oliver Goldsmith*

* * *

□ Lives of great men all remind us
We can make our lives sublime,
And departing, leave behind us
Footprints on the sands of time.
*Henry Wadsworth Longfellow*

* * *

□ Few things are harder to put up with than the annoyance of a good example.
*Mark Twain*

# Experience

□ I have but one lamp by which my feet are guided, and that is the lamp of experience.                                    *Patrick Henry*

* * *

□ What is experience? A poor little hut constructed from the ruins of the palace of gold and marble called our illusions.

*Joseph Roux*

# Failure

□ They fail, and they alone, who have not striven.

*Thomas Bailey Aldrich*

* * *

□ "All honor to him who shall win the prize,"
The world has cried for a thousand years;
But to him who tries and fails and dies,
I give great honor and glory and tears.

*Joaquin Miller*

# Fall

□ But yesterday, the word of Caesar might
Have stood against the world: now lies he there
And none so poor to do him reverence.

*Julius Caesar III*

# Fame

□ Fame is the thirst of youth.                                    *George Gordon*

* * *

□ The fame of men ought always to be estimated by the means used to acquire it.                    *Francois de La Rochefoucauld*

□ Fame is no sure test of merit, but only a probability of such: it is an accident, not a property of a man.     *Thomas Carlyle*

\* \* \*

□ Ah, pensive scholar, what is fame?
A fitful tongue of leaping flame;
A giddy whirlwind's fickle gust,
That lifts a pinch of mortal dust.
    *Oliver Wendell Holmes*

\* \* \*

□ And what after all is everlasting fame? Altogether vanity.
    *Marcus Aurelius*

\* \* \*

□ Fame due to the achievements of the mind never perishes.
    *Propertius*

# Farewell

□ So sweetly she bade me adieu,
I thought she bade me return.     *William Shenstone*

# Fate

□ Let us, then, be up and doing,
With a heart for any fate.
    *Henry Wadsworth Longfellow*

\* \* \*

□ Fate with impartial hand turns out the doom of high and low; her capacious urn is constantly shaking out the names of all mankind.     *Horace*

□ The Moving Finger writes; and having writ,
  Moves on; nor all your Piety nor Wit
  Shall lure it back to cancel half a Line,
  Nor all your Tears wash out a Word of it.
                                    *Edward Fitzgerald*

# Freedom

□ Freedom exists only where the people take care of the government.                                    *Woodrow Wilson*

# Friendship

□ We cannot tell the precise moment when friendship is formed. As in filling a vessel drop by drop, there is at last a drop which makes it run over; so in a series of kindnesses there is at last one which makes the heart run over.                    *James Boswell*

\* \* \*

□ A true friend is somebody who can make us do what we can.
                                    *Ralph Waldo Emerson*

# Futility

□ I have spent my life laboriously doing nothing.    *Hugo Grotius*

\* \* \*

□ He has spent all his life in letting down empty buckets into empty wells; and he is frittering away his age in trying to draw them up again.                                    *Sydney Smith*

# Future

□ No man can tell what the future may bring forth.    *Demosthenes*

205

◻ No one can walk backwards into the future.

*Joseph Hergesheimer*

\* \* \*

◻ Tomorrow, and tomorrow, and tomorrow,
Creeps in this petty pace from day to day
To the last syllable of recorded time.

*William Shakespeare*

# Gain

◻ Everywhere in life, the true question is not what we gain, but what we do.  *Thomas Carlyle*

# Gambling

◻ We should all be concerned about the future because we will have to spend the rest of our lives there.  *Charles F. Kettering*

# Genius

◻ Doing easily what others find difficult is talent; doing what is impossible for talent is genius.  *Henri-Frederic Amiel*

\* \* \*

◻ Genius is mainly an affair of energy.  *Matthew Arnold*

\* \* \*

◻ Talent may be in time forgiven, but genius never!

*George Gordon*

# Goodness

☐ That best portion of a good man's life,—
　His little, nameless, unremembered acts
　Of kindness and of love. *William Wordsworth*

# Gratitude

☐ Gratitude is a fruit of great cultivation; you do not find it among gross people. *Samuel Johnson*

# Greatness

☐ The price of greatness is responsibility. *Winston Churchill*

\* \* \*

☐ Rough is the road that leads to the heights of greatness. *Seneca*

\* \* \*

☐ Great hopes make great men. *Thomas Fuller*

\* \* \*

☐ Great lives never go out. They go on. *Benjamin Harrison*

# Happiness

☐ The happiness of men consists in life. And life is labor.
*Leo Tolstoy*

# Heroes

□ A hero is no braver than an ordinary man, but he is brave five minutes longer. *Ralph Waldo Emerson*

# Hope

□ Hope springs eternal in the human breast;
Man never is, but always to be blest.
*Alexander Pope*

# Humility

□ Humility, that low, sweet root
From which all heavenly virtues shoot.
*Thomas Moore*

\* \* \*

□ Humility is the most difficult of all virtues to achieve; nothing dies harder than the desire to think well of oneself. *T. S. Eliot*

\* \* \*

□ Humility like darkness reveals the heavenly lights.
*Henry D. Thoreau*

# Ideals

□ Our ideals are our better selves. *Amos Bronson Alcott*

# Idleness

□ He did nothing in particular,
And did it very well.

*Sir William S. Gilbert*

□ Too much rest is rust. *Sir Walter Scott*

# Ignorance

□ To be conscious that you are ignorant is a great step to knowledge. *Benjamin Disraeli*

# Industry

□ In the ordinary business of life, industry can do anything which genius can do, and very many things which it cannot.
*Henry Ward Beecher*

# Knowledge

□ Every addition to true knowledge is an addition to human power. *Horace Mann*

\* \* \*

□ Each of June's new graduates
Has left his college hall.
The world is now his oyster,
The future is his thrall.
He thinks he knows a great, great deal
More than his parents do—
And, speaking of that state of mind,
The chances are it's true!

*Leverett Lyon*

\* \* \*

□ It is the province of knowledge to speak, and it is the privilege of wisdom to listen. *Oliver Wendell Holmes*

# Language

□ Language is the dress of thought.              *Samuel Johnson*

# Laughter

□ If life were always merry,
Our souls would seek relief
And rest from weary laughter
In the quiet arms of grief.

*Henry van Dyke*

\* \* \*

□ Laugh and the world laughs with you
Weep and you weep alone,
For the sad old earth must borrow its mirth,
But has trouble enough of its own.

*Ella Wheeler Wilcox*

# Law

□ Law is a pledge that the citizens of a state will do justice to one another.              *Aristotle*

# Learning

□ A little learning is a dangerous thing;
Drink deep, or taste not the Pierian spring:
There shallow draughts intoxicate the brain,
And drinking largely sobers us again.

*Alexander Pope*

# Life

□ Life is made up of sobs, sniffles, and smiles, with sniffles predominating.              *O. Henry*

❑ Only a life lived for others is a life worth while. *Albert Einstien*

\* \* \*

❑ God asks no man whether he will accept life. That is not the choice. You must take it. The only choice is how.

*Henry Ward Beecher*

\* \* \*

❑ Tell me not, in mournful numbers,
Life is but an empty dream! *Henry Wadsworth Longfellow*

\* \* \*

❑ There is nothing of which men are so fond, and withal so careless, as life. *Jean de La Bruyere*

\* \* \*

❑ The web of our life is of a mingled yarn, good and ill together.
*William Shakespeare*

# Memory

❑ Where is the heart that doth not keep,
Within its inmost core,
Some fond remembrance hidden deep,
Of days that are no more?
*Ellen Clementine Howarth*

\* \* \*

❑ How sweet to remember the trouble that is past. *Euripides*

# Mind

❑ The empires of the future are empires of the mind.
*Winston Churchill*

□ The mind is the soul's eye, not its source of power: that lies in the heart.                                    *Marquis de Vauvenargues*

# Nobility

□ There is a natural aristocracy among men.
The grounds of this are virtue and talents.
                                    *Thomas Jefferson*

\* \* \*

□ Be noble! and the nobleness that lies
In other men, sleeping, but never dead,
Will rise in majesty to meet thine own.
                                    *James Russell Lowell*

# Opinion

□ The only sin which we never forgive in each other is difference of opinion.                                    *Ralph Waldo Emerson*

\* \* \*

□ The average man believes a thing first, and then searches for proof to bolster his opinion.                *Elbert Hubbard*

\* \* \*

□ Error of opinion may be tolerated where reason is left free to combat it.                                    *Thomas Jefferson*

\* \* \*

□ Too often we . . . enjoy the comfort of opinion without the discomfort of thought.                        *John F. Kennedy*

# Opportunity

☐ Seize now and here the hour that is, nor trust some later day.

*Horace*

\* \* \*

☐ Each is given a bag of tools,
A shapeless mass,
A book of rules,
And each must make
Ere life has flown
A stumbling block
Or a stepping stone.

*R. L. Sharpe*

\* \* \*

☐ We sail, at sunrise, daily, "outward bound."

*Helen Hunt Jackson*

\* \* \*

☐ There is no security on this earth; there is only opportunity.

*General Douglas MacArthur*

\* \* \*

☐ They do me wrong who say I come no more
When once I knock and fail to find you in;
For every day I stand outside your door
And bid you wake, and rise to fight and win.

*Walter Malone*

# Optimism

☐ The optimist proclaims that we live in the best of all possible worlds; and the pessimest fears this is true.

*James Branch Cabell*

# Oratory

□ I sometimes marvel at the extraordinary docility with which Americans submit to speeches. *Adlai E. Stevenson*

# Pain

□ Pain makes man think. Thought makes man wise. Wisdom makes life endurable. *John Patrick*

\* \* \*

□ No pain, no palm; no thorn, no throne. *William Penn*

\* \* \*

□ Let's tell them (the American people) the truth, that there are no gains without pains. *Adlai E. Stevenson*

# Past

□ I know of no way of judging the future but by the past. *Patrick Henry*

\* \* \*

□ The dogmas of the quiet past are inadequate to the stormy present. *Abraham Lincoln*

\* \* \*

□ Those who cannot remember the past are condemned to repeat it. *George Santayana*

\* \* \*

□ Look not mournfully into the Past. It comes not back again. Wisely improve the Present. It is thine. Go forth to meet the shadowy Future, without fear, and with a manly heart. *Henry Wadsworth Longfellow*

# Patriotism

□ And so, my fellow Americans: ask not what your country can do for you—ask what you can do for your country.

*John F. Kennedy*

* * *

□ The patriots are those who love America enough to wish to see her as a model to mankind. *Adlai E. Stevenson*

* * *

□ There are misguided patriots who feel we pay too much attention to other nations, that we are somehow enfeebled by respecting world opinion. . . . The founding fathers did not think it was "soft" or "un-American" to respect the opinions of others, and today for a man to love his country truly, he must also know how to love mankind.

# Peace

□ Our understanding of how to live—live with one another—is still far behind our knowledge of how to destroy one another.

*Lyndon B. Johnson*

* * *

□ The focus of the problem does not lie in the atom; it resides in the hearts of men. *Henry L. Stimson*

# Peace of Mind

□ To be glad of life because it gives you the chance to love and to work and to play and to look up at the stars, to be satisfied with your possessions but not contented with yourself until you have made the best of them, to despise nothing in the world except falsehood and meanness and to fear nothing except cowardice, to be governed by your admirations rather than by your disgusts, to covet nothing that is your neighbor's except his kindness of heart and gentleness of manners, to think seldom of your enemies, often of your friends, and every day of Christ, and to spend as much time as you can, with body and with spirit, in God's out-of-doors, these are little guideposts on the footpath to peace.

*Henry van Dyke*

# Perseverance

☐ The heights by great men reached and kept
Were not attained by sudden flight,
But they, while their companions slept,
Were toiling upward in the night.

*Henry Wadsworth Longfellow*

* * *

☐ And many strokes, though with a little axe,
Hew down and fell the hardest-timbered oak.

*William Shakespeare*

# Personality

☐ I am bigger than anything that can happen to me. All these things, sorrow, misfortune, and suffering, are outside my door. I am in the house and I have a key.     *Charles F. Lummis*

# Philosophy

☐ Philosophy is common-sense in a dress suit.     *Oliver S. Braston*

* * *

☐ The society which scorns excellence in plumbing because plumbing is a humble activity and tolerates shoddiness in philosophy because it is an exalted activity will have neither good plumbing nor good philosophy. Neither its pipes nor its theories will hold water.     *John W. Gardner*

# Pity

☐ Give plenty of what is given to you,
Listen to pity's call;
Don't think the little you give is great,
And the much you get is small.

*Phoebe Cary*

# Possessions

☐ You give but little when you give of your possessions. It is when you give of yourself that you truly give.   *Kahlil Gibran*

# Prayer

☐ Do not pray for easy lives. Pray to be stronger men. Do not pray for tasks equal to your power. Pray for powers equal to you tasks.   *Phillips Brooks*

# Prejudice

☐ Ignorance is stubborn and prejudice dies hard.

*Adlai E. Stevenson*

\* \* \*

☐ Prejudice is the child of ignorance.   *William Hazlitt*

# Present

☐ Our todays and yesterdays
Are the blocks with which we build.

*Henry Wadsworth Longfellow*

# Price

☐ Wisdom is never dear, provided the article be genuine.

*Horace Greeley*

# Principle

□ It is often easier to fight for principles than to live up to them.
*Adlai E. Stevenson*

# Prize

□ Have you something to do tomorrow; do it today.
*Benjamin Franklin*

# Procrastination

□ Procrastination is the
art of keeping up with yesterday.
*Don Marquis*

\* \* \*

□ While we are procrastinating life speeds by.
*Seneca*

# Progress

□ Life means progress, and progress means suffering.
*Hendrik Willem van Loon*

\* \* \*

□ And step by step, since time began,
I see the steady gain of man.
*John Greenleaf Whittier*

# Prudence

□ Who never wins can rarely lose,
Who never climbs as rarely falls.
*John Greenleaf Whittier*

# Reading

□ Our high respect for a well-read man is praise enough of literature. *Ralph Waldo Emerson*

\* \* \*

□ Reading makes a full man—meditation a profound man—
discourse a clear man. *Benjamin Franklin*

# Reason

□ Reason never has failed men. Only force and oppression have
made the wrecks in the world. *William Allen White*

\* \* \*

□ Reason, the choicest gift bestowed by heaven. *Sophocles*

# Regret

□ For of all sad words of tongue or pen,
   The saddest are these: "It might have been!"
                  *John Greenleaf Whittier*

\* \* \*

□ If, of all sad words of tongue or pen,
   The saddest are, "It might have been,"
   More sad are these we daily see,
   "It is, but it hadn't ought to be."

                  *Bret Harte*

# Resolution

□ Let us, then, be up and doing,
   With a heart for any fate;

Still achieving, still pursuing,
Learn to labor and to wait.
*Henry Wadsworth Longfellow*

\* \* \*

☐ In life's small things be resolute and great
To keep they muscle trained: know'st thou
when Fate
Thy measure takes, or when she'll say to
thee,
"I find thee worthy; do this deed for me"?
*James Russell Lowell*

# Reward

☐ The highest reward for man's toil is not what he gets for it but what he becomes by it. *John Ruskin*

# Riches

☐ Riches are not an end to life but an instrument of life.
*Henry Ward Beecher*

\* \* \*

☐ Few rich men own their own property. The property owns them. *Robert Ingersoll*

# Rights

☐ Let us have faith that right makes might, and in that faith let us to the end dare to do our duty as we understand it.
*Abraham Lincoln*

□ I believe that every right implies a responsibility; every opportunity, an obligation; every possession, a duty.

*John D. Rockefeller, Jr.*

# Scholar

□ The scholar who cherishes the love of comfort is not fit to be deemed a scholar. *Confucius*

\* \* \*

□ A scholar is the favorite of Heaven and earth, the excellency of his country, the happiest of men. *Ralph Waldo Emerson*

\* \* \*

□ It does not necessarily follow that a scholar in the humanities is also a humanist—but it should. For what does it avail a man to be the greatest expert on John Donne if he cannot hear the bell tolling? *Milton S. Eisenhower*

# Sculpture

□ A sculptor wields
The chisel, and the stricken marble grows
To beauty.

*William Cullen Bryant*

# Self-Confidence

□ It matters not how strait the gate,
How charged with punishments the scroll,
I am the master of my fate;
I am the captain of my soul.

*William Ernest Henley*

221

# Self-Control

□ No conflict is so severe as his who labors to subdue himself.

*Thomas A. Kempis*

\* \* \*

□ But I will write of him who fights,
And vanquishes his sins,
Who struggles on through weary years
Against himself and wins.

*Caroline Le Row*

# Self-Knowledge

□ Make it thy business to know thyself, which is the most difficult lesson in the world.                *Miguel de Cervantes*

\* \* \*

□ To thine own self be true,
And it must follow, as the night the day,
Thou canst not then be false to any man.

*William Shakespeare*

\* \* \*

□ Great God, I ask thee for no meaner pelf
Than that I may not disappoint myself.

*Henry David Thoreau*

# Service

□ I prefer death to lassitude. I never tire of serving others.

*Leonardo da Vinci*

□ We are here to add what we can to, not to get what we can from, life. *Sir William Osler*

* * *

□ This is man's highest end,
   To others' service all his powers to bend.
                                          *Sophocles*

* * *

□ The vocation of every man and woman is to serve other people.
                                          *Leo Tolstoy*

# Simplicity

□ There are some things which cannot be learned quickly, and time, which is all we have, must be paid heavily for their acquiring. They are the very simplest things and because it takes a man's life to know them the little new that each man gets from life is very costly and the only heritage he has to leave. *Ernest Hemingway*

* * *

□ Nothing is more simple than greatness; indeed, to be simple is to be great. *Ralph Waldo Emerson*

# Solitude

□ That inward eye which is the bliss of solitude.
                                          *William Wordsworth*

# Soul

□ Build thee more stately mansions, O my soul.
                                          *Oliver Wendell Holmes*

□ I am the captain of my soul;
I rule it with stern joy;
And yet I think I had more fun
When I was a cabin boy.

*Keith Preston*

\* \* \*

□ Out of the night that covers me,
Black as the pit from pole to pole,
I thank whatever gods may be
For my unconquerable soul.

*William Ernest Henley*

# Speech

□ Blessed is the man who having nothing to say abstains from giving us wordy evidence of the fact.  *George Eliot*

\* \* \*

□ The first principle of a free society is an untrammeled flow of words in an open forum.  *Adlai E. Stevenson*

# Sport

□ For when the One Great Scorer comes to
write against your name,
He marks—not that you won or lost—but
how you played the game.

*Grantland Rice*

# Strength

□ We acquire the strength we have overcome.

*Ralph Waldo Emerson*

◻ But noble souls, through dust and heat,
　Rise from disaster and defeat
　The stronger.

*Henry Wadsworth Longfellow*

# Stupidity

◻ A thick head can do as much damage as a hard heart.

*Harold Willis Dodds*

\* \* \*

◻ It is the dull man who is always sure, and the sure man who is always dull.

*H. L. Mencken*

# Success

◻ The toughest things about success is that you've got to keep on being a success.

*Irving Berlin*

\* \* \*

◻ He started to sing as he tackled the thing
　That couldn't be done, and he did it.

*Edgar A. Guest*

\* \* \*

◻ Failure is often that early morning hour of darkness which precedes the dawning of the day of success.

*Leigh Mitchell Hodges*

\* \* \*

The talent of success is nothing more than doing what you can do well; and doing well whatever you do, without a thought of fame.

*Henry Wadsworth Longfellow*

◻ Not in the clamor of the crowded street,
Not in the shouts and plaudits of the throng,
But in ourselves, are triumph and defeat.

*Henry Wadsworth Longfellow*

# Suffering

◻ For he who much has suffer'd, much will know.         *Homer*

# Superiority

◻ There are three marks of superior man: being virtuous, he is free from anxiety; being wise, he is free from perplexity; being brave, he is free from fear.         *Confucius*

# Talent

◻ If a man has a talent and cannot use it, he has failed. If he has a talent and uses only half of it, he has partly failed. If he has a talent and learns somehow to use the whole of it, he has gloriously succeeded, and won a satisfaction and a triumph few men ever know.         *Thomas Wolfe*

# Teaching

◻ For him the teacher's chair became a throne.

*Henry Wadsworth Longfellow*

\* \* \*

◻ A teacher affects eternity; he can never tell where his influence stops.         *Henry Adams*

# Thought

◻ During my eighty-seven years I have witnessed a whole succession of technological revolutions. But none of them has done away with the need for character in the individual or the ability to think.                                                    *Bernard M. Baruch*

\* \* \*

□ Thinking is the hardest work there is, which is the probable reason why so few engage in it.                              *Henry Ford*

\* \* \*

□ They are never alone that are accompanied with noble thoughts.
*Sir Philip Sidney*

\* \* \*

□ Mind is the great lever of all things; human thought is the process by which all human ends are ultimately answered.
*Daniel Webster*

\* \* \*

□ There is no expedient to which a man will not go to avoid the real labor of thinking.                          *Thomas A. Edison*

\* \* \*

□ Beware when the great God lets loose a thinker on this planet.
*Ralph Walso Emerson*

\* \* \*

□ What is the hardest task in the world? To think.
*Ralph Walso Emerson*

\* \* \*

□ And what they dare to dream of, dare to do.
*James Russell Lowell*

\* \* \*

□ He was the man of thought in an age of action.   *James Reston*

# Time

□ Alas! how swift the moments fly!
How flash the years along!
Scarce here, yet gone already by,
The burden of a song.
See childhood, youth, and manhood pass,
And age with furrowed brow;
Time was—Time shall be—drain the glass—
But where in Time is now?

*John Quincy Adams*

\* \* \*

□ There's a time for some things, and a time for all things; a time
for great things, and a time for small things.

*Miguel de Cervantes Saavedra*

\* \* \*

□ It is the wisest who grieve most at loss of time.   *Dante Alighieri*

\* \* \*

□ Nothing is so dear and precious as time.   *Francois Rebelais*

\* \* \*

□ The small intolerable drums
Of Time are like slow drops descending.

*Edwin Arlington Robinson*

\* \* \*

□ Ah! the clock is always slow;
It is later than you think.

*Robert William Service*

\* \* \*

□ What is time? The shadow on the dial, the striking of the clock,
the running of the sand, day and night, summer and winter,

months, years, centuries—these are but arbitrary and outward signs, the measure of Time, not Time itself. Time is the Life of the soul.                                        *Henry Wadsworth Longfellow*

\* \* \*

□ Whether or not we admit it to ourselves, we are all haunted by a truly awful sense of impermanence.          *Tennessee Williams*

\* \* \*

□ The time God allots to each one of us is like a precious tissue which we embroider as we best know how.          *Anatole France*

\* \* \*

□ See how the generations pass
  Like sand through Heaven's blue hour-glass.
                                        *Vachel Lindsay*

\* \* \*

□ Time is lord of thee:
  Thy wealth, thy glory, and thy name are his.
                                        *Thomas Love Peacock*

\* \* \*

□ Backward, turn backward, O time, in your flight,
  Make me a child again just for tonight.
                                        *Elizabeth Akers Allen*

\* \* \*

□ The rust will find the sword of fame,
  The dust will hide the crown;
  Ay, none shall nail so high his name
  Time will not tear it down.
                                        *John Vance Cheney*

# Transitoriness of Things

◻ Riches have wings, and grandeur is a dream.     *William Cowper*

# Trouble

◻ Oh, a trouble's a ton, or a trouble's an ounce,
Or a trouble is what you make it.
And it isn't the fact that you're hurt that counts,
But only how did you take it?
                              *Edmund Vance Cooke*

# Truth

◻ It is a question of searching for truth by the light of the scholar's lamp in the study, not by the light of a torch at the barricades.
                              *Bernard S. Adams*

# University

◻ It is . . . a small college, and yet there are those that love it.
                              *Daniel Webster*

# Wisdom

◻ Great is wisdom; infinite is the value of wisdom. It cannot be exaggerated; it is the highest achievement of man.
                              *Thomas Carlyle*

* * *

◻ Much of the wisdom of the world is not wisdom.
                              *Ralph Waldo Emerson*

230

# Woman

> □ And still they gazed, and still the wonder grew,
> That one small head should carry all it knew.
>
> *Oliver Goldsmith*

# Work

> □ Work is love made visible.  *Kahlil Gibran*

\* \* \*

> □ Toil, says the proverb, is the sire of fame.  *Euripides*

\* \* \*

> □ And only The Master shall praise us,
> and only The Master shall blame;
> And no one shall work for money,
> and no one shall work for fame;
> But each for the joy of the working,
> and each in his separate star,
> Shall draw the Thing as he sees it
> for the God of Things as They are!
>
> *Rudyard Kipling*

\* \* \*

> □ Don't worry and fret, fain-hearted,
> The chances have just begun,
> For the best jobs haven't been started,
> The best work hasn't been done.
>
> *Berton Braley*

\* \* \*

> □ With a good conscience our only sure reward, with history the
> final judge of our deeds, let us go forth to lead the land we love,

asking His blessing and His help, but knowing that here on earth
God's work must truly be our own.          *John F. Kennedy*

\* \* \*

□ Serve and thou shalt be served. If you love and serve men, you
cannot, by any hiding or stratagem, escape the remuneration.
*Ralph Waldo Emerson*

\* \* \*

□ Each morning sees some task begin,
  Each evening sees it close;
  Something attempted, something done,
  Has earned a night's repose.
*Henry Wadsworth Longfellow*

# World

□ All the world's a stage,
  And all the men and women merely players;
  They have their exits and their entrances;
  And one man in his time plays many parts.
*William Shakespeare*

\* \* \*

□ The world is too much with us; late and soon,
  Getting and spending, we lay waste our powers.
*William Wordsworth*

# Year

□ In masks outrageous and austere
  The years go by in single file;
  But none has merited my fear,
  And none has quite escaped my smile.
*Elinor Wylie*

☐ Truth forever on the scaffold,
Wrong forever on the throne.
*James Russell Lowell*

# Youth

☐ Towering in the confidence of twenty-one.     *Samuel Johnson*

\* \* \*

☐ How beautiful is youth! how bright it gleams
With its illusions, aspirations, dreams!
Book of beginnings, story without end,
Each maid a heroine, and each man a friend!
*Henry Wadsworth Longfellow*

# Part Six

---

## INSPIRING
## AND
## THOUGHTFUL
## OBSERVATIONS

# Mud, or Beauty?

◻ When Lincoln Steffens was a boy, he watched an artist at work painting a picture of a muddy river. He criticized the picture because there was so much "mud" in it, to which the artist replied: "You see the mud in the picture, my boy. All right, there is mud, and lots of it. But I see the beautiful colors and contrasts, the beautiful harmonies, and the light as against the dark."

"Mud or beauty—which do we look for as we journey through life?" later sermonized Mr. Steffens. "If we look for mud and ugliness, we find them—they are there. If we look for beauty, character, nobility, we find them, too. Just as the artist found beauty in the muddy river, because that is what he was looking for, we will find, in the stream of life, those things which we desire to see. To look for the best and see the beautiful is the way to get the best out of life each day."  *Sunshine Magazine*

# Aspiration

◻ Did you ever hear of a man who had striven all his life faithfully and singly towards an object, and in no measure obtained it? If a man constantly aspires, is he not elevated? Did ever a man try heroism, magnanimity, truth, sincerity, and find that there was no advantage in them—that it was a vain endeavor?

*Henry David Thoreau*

# Holds True of Many Things

◻ One night in ancient times, three horsemen were riding across a desert. A voice in the darkness called out to them to halt and dismount. When they had dismounted the voice told them to fill their pockets with pebbles. They did as the voice ordered. And then the voice commanded them to mount and ride on. As they started off into the darkness the voice predicted that they would be both glad and sorry that they had stopped. The three horsemen rode on through the darkness. When the night faded into dawn they reined in their horses and examined the pebbles that they had picked up. They found the "pebbles" to be precious jewels ... and, as the voice had predicted, they were both glad and sorry. Glad that they had taken some ... and sorry that they had not taken more. *Jacob F. Bryan III*

# Books

❑ I go into my library, and all history unrolls before me. I breathe the morning air of the world while the scent of Eden's roses yet lingered in it, while it vibrated only to the world's first brood of nightingales, and to the laugh of Eve. I see the pyramids building; I hear the shoutings of the armies of Alexander.

*Alexander Smith*

\* \* \*

❑ Live always in the best company when you read. *Sydney Smith*

# Reading

❑ For what are the classics but the noblest recorded thoughts of man? They are the only oracles which are not decayed.

*Henry David Thoreau*

\* \* \*

❑ Have you ever rightly considered what the mere ability to read means? That it is the key which admits us to the whole world of thought and fancy and imagination? to the company of saint and sage, of the wisest and the wittiest at their wisest and wittiest moment? That it enables us to see with the keenest eyes, hear with the finest ears, and listen to the sweetest voices of all time?

*James Russell Lowell*

## Fight It Out

□ You cannot run away from a weakness; you must some time fight it out or perish; and if that be so, why not now, and where you stand?

*Robert Louis Stevenson*

## America

□ America! America!
God shed His grace on thee
And crown thy good with brotherhood
From sea to shining sea!

*Katharine Lee Bates*

\* \* \*

□ Bring me men to match my mountains;
Bring me men to match my plains,
Men with empires in their purpose,
And new ears in their brains.

*Sam Walter Foss*

\* \* \*

□ My God! how little do my countrymen know what precious blessings they are in possession of, and which no other people on earth enjoy!

*Thomas Jefferson*

\* \* \*

□ I believe in the United States of America as a government of the people, by the people, for the people, whose just powers are derived from the consent of the governed; a democracy in a republic; a sovereign nation of many sovereign states; a perfect union, one and inseparable; established upon those principles of freedom, equality, justice, and humanity for which American patriots sacrificed their lives and fortunes. I therefore believe it is my duty to my country to love it, to support its constitution, to obey its laws, to respect its flag, and to defend it against all enemies. *William Tyler Page*

\* \* \*

□ Let our object be, our country, our whole country, and nothing but our country. And, by the blessing of God, may that country itself become a vast and splendid monument, not of oppression and terror, but of wisdom, of peace, and of liberty, upon which the world may gaze with admiration forever. *Daniel Webster*

\* \* \*

□ America lives in the heart of every man everywhere who wishes to find a region where he will be free to work out his destiny as he chooses. *Woodrow Wilson*

\* \* \*

□ For this is what America is all about. It is the uncrossed desert and the unclimbed ridge. It is the star that is not reached and the harvest that's sleeping in the unplowed ground.
*Lyndon B. Johnson*

\* \* \*

□ What constitutes the bulwark of our own liberty and independence? It is not our frowning battlements, our bristling sea coasts. . . . Our reliance is in the love of liberty which God has planted in us. Our defense is in the spirit which prized liberty as the heritage of all men, in all lands everywhere. *Abraham Lincoln*

# Civilization

□ A civilization which develops only on its material side, and not in corresponding measure on its mental and spiritual side, is like a vessel with a defective steering gear, which gets out of control at a constantly accelerating pace, and drifts toward catastrophe.

*Albert Schweitzer*

* * *

□ A decent provision for the poor is the true test of civilization.

*Samuel Johnson*

# Quarreling

□ Greatly begin! Though thou have time
But for a line, be that sublime—
Not failure, but low aim is crime.

*James Russell Lowell*

# It Is the Day of ...

□ This school has labored since 1780 to equip young people to meet the world around them. Young people prepared with skills for earning a living and imbued with a Christian faith in God and his servant, man, have found their place in their day. What kind of day is today? Well, it's a new day in education. It is the day of:

academic opportunity and TV euphoria
remedial reading and the new math
a man headed for the moon and the dropout headed for the
  pool hall
two cars in every garage and school breakfasts for the children
the educational city on the drawing board and board windows
  on the neighborhood schools
affluent urbanity and rural poverty
the walk in space and the Civil Rights march
LSD and no prayers in schools
"The Greatest Story Ever Told" and "Who's Afraid of Virginia
  Woolf"
Billy Graham and Batman
White Backlash and Black Power
unemployment compensation and color TV in the living room
the industrial merger and the isolated country store

241

the city commuter and the empty barn on the farm
billion dollar annual sales and small business bankruptcy
the $100-a-plate dinner and the potluck church supper
instant foods and the backyard barbecue
God is dead and the Bible Belt
Yes, it is indeed a new day in education.

*T. Henry Jablonski,*
*President, Washington College Academy,*
*Washington College, Tennessee*

# Fame

□ Fame is the spur that the clear spirit doth raise
(That last infirmity of noble mind)
To scorn delights, and live laborious days;
But the fair guerdon when we hope to find,
And think to burst out into sudden blaze,
Comes the blind Fury with th' abhorred shears
And slits the thin-spun life.

*John Milton*

# Knowledge

□ "Knowledge is power." Yes, that is what knowledge is. It is power and nothing more. As a power it is like wealth, talent, or any power, that is, it is without any moral element whatever. The moral question always comes in when we ask, in respect to the man who has power: What will he do with it?

*William Graham Sumner*

# Self-Evaluation

□ I do not know what I may appear to the world; but to myself I seem to have been only like a boy playing on the seashore, and diverting myself in now and then finding a smoother pebble or a prettier shell than ordinary, whilst the great ocean of truth lay all undiscovered before me. *Sir Isaac Newton*

# What God Demands

□ The self we loved is not the self God loves,
the neighbors we did not prize
are His treasures, the truth we ignored
is the truth He maintains,
the justice which we sought because
it was our own is not the justice
that His love desires.
The righteousness He demands and gives
is not our righteousness but greater and
different. He requires of us the sacrifice
of all we would conserve and grants us
gifts we had not dreamed of.

*H. Richard Niebuhr*

# Democracy

□ One of the most difficult decisions the individual in a democracy faces is whether or not he should forgo an immediate personal gain or advantage for the good of his country.

*Dwight D. Eisenhower*

\* \* \*

□ The world will little note nor long remember what we say here, but it can never forget what they did here. . . . It is rather for us to be here dedicated to the great task remaining before us—that from these honored dead we take increased devotion to that cause for which they gave the last full measure of devotion; that we here highly resolve that these dead shall not have died in vain; that this nation, under God, shall have a new birth of freedom; and that the government of the people, by the people, for the people, shall not perish from the earth.          *Abraham Lincoln*

# Failure

□ Men do not fail; they give up trying.          *Elihu Root*

# Your Aspiration

□ If you aspire to the highest place, it is no disgrace to stop at the second, or even the third.                                                    *Cicero*

# Old Gaelic Blessing

□ May the roads rise with you,
  And the wind be always at your back;
  And may the Lord hold you in the hollow of His hand.

# Profanity

□ There is a profanity in words, and we need to be cautious about that, but again words are simply a clue to a deeper disease. How do you deal with profanity?

Jim Bishop, the syndicated columnist, gives one answer in this tender story: It happened on a street corner where a group of people had gathered to wait for a bus. Nearby some laborers were working and talking loudly to each other. One of them was using a sordid array of vulgar adjectives and profanity in his conversation; his vocabulary was so rough that even the men bystanders were embarrassed. The columnist says that a little, blue-eyed elderly lady finally walked over to the workman and said sweetly, "Mister, you must know God very well for you use His Name so familiarly!" It was a gentle rebuke.

*The Reverend Ernest J. Lewis*

# Mind

□ If we work upon marble, it will perish. If we work upon brass, time will efface it. If we rear temples, they will crumble to dust. But if we work upon men's immortal minds, if we imbue them with high principles, with the just fear of God and love of their fellowmen, we engrave on those tablets something which no time can efface, and which will brighten and brighten to all eternity.

*Daniel Webster*

# Individuality

◻ Individualism is a fatal poison. But individuality is the salt of common life. You may have to live in a crowd, but you do not have to live like it, nor subsist on its food. You may have your own orchard. You may drink at a hidden spring. Be yourself if you would serve others. *Henry van Dyke*

# Poverty

◻ We in America today are nearer to the final triumph over poverty than ever before in the history of any land. The poorhouse is vanishing from among us. *Herbert Hoover*

# Experience

◻ Experience keeps a dear school, but fools will learn in no other. *Benjamin Franklin*

\* \* \*

◻ I have but one lamp by which my feet are guided, and that is the lamp of experience. I know of no way of judging of the future but by the past. *Patrick Henry*

# Honor

◻ When faith is lost, when honor dies,
The man is dead!

*John Greenleaf Whittier*

# Human Nature

◻ Human action can be modified to some extent, but human nature cannot be changed. *Abraham Lincoln*

245

◻ You must not lose faith in humanity. Humanity is an ocean; if a few drops of the ocean are dirty, the ocean does not become dirty.

*Gandhi*

# Aspiration

◻ Make no little plans: they have no magic to stir men's blood . . . . Make big plans, aim high in hope and work.

*Daniel H. Burnham*

\* \* \*

◻ Carve your name on hearts and not on marble.

*Charles Haddon Spurgeon*

# The Eagle and the Oyster

◻ When God made the oyster, He guaranteed him economic and social security. He built the oyster a house, a shell to protect him. When hungry, the oyster simply opens his shell and food rushes in. But when God made the eagle, He said, "The blue sky is the limit. Build your own house." So the eagle built on the highest mountain where storms threaten every day. For food, he flies through miles of rain and snow and wind. The eagle, not the oyster, is the emblem of America.

# Humility

◻ Humility is the solid function of all virtues.        *Confucius*

\* \* \*

◻ The most thankful people are the humblest.

\* \* \*

◻ I believe the first test of a truly great man is his humility.

*John Ruskin*

# Character

□ Virtue may not always make a face handsome but vice will certainly make it ugly. *Benjamin Franklin*

# Fame

□ The man who wakes up and find himself famous hasn't been asleep.

# Man

□ I believe that man will not merely endure: he will prevail. He is immortal, not because he alone among creatures has an inexhaustible voice, but because he has a soul, a spirit capable of compassion and sacrifice and endurance. *William Faulkner*

# Hold Fast

□ Tired
And lonely,
So tired
The heart aches
Down the rocks,
The fingers are numb,
The knees tremble,
It is now,
Now, that you must not give in.

*Dag Hammarskjold*

# Today

□ My favorite slogan is "Today is the first day of the rest of your life." So it's no use fussing about the past because you can't do anything about it. But you have today, and today is when everything that's going to happen from now on begins.

*Harvey Firestone, Jr.*

# Conscience

☐ Labour to keep alive in your breast that little spark of celestial fire, conscience. *George Washington*

# Failure

☐ Failure, even if it be a plain, unvarnished, complete failure, has a certain dignity, because it is a monument to the fact that a man tried to do something.

Failure is sometimes necessary to show us we are headed in the wrong direction. We can use our mistakes as a source of instruction. Instead of dwelling upon explanations and excuses, admit it, rectify it, and push on. As Churchill said: "If you simply take up the attitude of defending it there will be no hope of improvement."

There is a class of persons called futilitarians, people who try to do this or that, but their efforts are futile. By and by they resign themselves to failure. Resignation is seldom the answer to any problem. What is needed is to go back before the beginning of the project and examine your thinking and action step by step in search of the point at which something can be done better.

Recall what the ghost said to the hesitating Hamlet: "This visitation is but to whet thy almost blunted purpose." And think of the poet Shelley. His biographer tells us that Shelley made a blot at the top of a page, but on the rest of the page he wrote a lovely poem. And consider the courage and determination of the Greek youth who was thrown from his chariot in a race recounted in the Iliad. He completed the course on foot, pulling his chariot behind him. *The Royal Bank of Canada Monthly letter*

# Self-Respect

☐ I desire so to conduct the affairs of this administration that if at the end, when I come to lay down the reins of power, I have lost every other friend on earth, I shall at least have one friend left, and that friend shall be down inside of me. *Abraham Lincoln*

# Generosity

◻ Generosity should never exceed ability.                    *Cicero*

# A Cause

◻ No matter what your age or job in life, you are more mature if you have found a "cause" in which to invest your time and money for some social good. Through it you can achieve an outstanding characteristic of emotional maturity—the ability to find satisfaction in giving.                    *Dr. William Menninger*

# Self-Restraint

◻ The finest command of language is often shown by saying nothing.                    *Rober Babson*

# Faith

◻ No ray of sunlight is ever lost, but the green which it awakes into existence needs time to sprout, and it is not always granted to the sower to see the harvest. All work that is worth anything is done in faith.                    *Albert Schweitzer*

# On Gifts

◻ Presents, I often say, endear absents.                    *Charles Lamb*

# Greatness and Ease

◻ The great ages of mankind, the ages of the most radical changes and the longest advances, the ages that later generations of men called great, were not the times of easy optimism when men thought everything discovered, everything architected, everything finished. Greatness and ease, vast innovation and untroubled stability are no more compatible among nations or in a world community than they are among individuals.     *Caryl P. Haskins*

# Liberty

□ The God who gave us life, gave us liberty at the same time.
*Thomas Jefferson*

# Endless Attaining

□ Efficiency involves endless attaining, the pleasure of inexhaustible transfiguration into better ways of doing things. It is the natural outcome of clear thinking, calm judgment, self-control, symmetry of planning, and artistry of means.

Your purpose in pursuing the philosophy of efficiency is to find the part you are to play on life's stage; to assure yourself that you are doing the work for which you are best endowed; to know that you are filling a vital need; to make certain that you are meeting your obligations effectively. This search for efficiency will prevent you from becoming merely an embodied function.

And then, having pushed up to a state of efficiency, you need to call upon a new resource, that of standing firmly. There is an appropriate parable in Rome. The Capitoline Hill was where consuls were sworn into office and victorious generals were crowned. At its edge was the Tarpeian Rock, from which criminals and traitors were cast down. Hence arose the saying: "It is not far from the Capitoline Hill to the Tarpeian Rock."
*The Royal Bank of Canada Monthly Letter*

# Do It Now

□ Perhaps the most valuable result of all education is the ability to make yourself do the thing you have to do, when it ought to be done, as it ought to be done, whether you like to do it or not.
*Thomas Huxley*

# A Faith to Live By

□ To some people in this age of science, the idea of "faith" seems out-of-date. Yet, as Arthur H. Compton said, "Faith gives the courage to live and do. Scientists with their disciplined thinking, like others, need a basis for the good life, for aspirations, for courage to do great deeds. They need a faith to live by. The hope of the world lies in those who have such faith and who use the methods of science to make their visions become real. Visions and hope and faith are not part of science. They are beyond the nature that science knows. Of such is the religion that gives meaning to life."

# Power

□ The United States is the least imperialistic of any nation who ever wielded super power. The Americans just want to get home to baseball and Coca-Cola. *Lester B. Pearson*

# Do It All the Time

□ An editor sent a letter to several hundred men and women who had "arrived" in their particular lines. He asked this question: "What do you consider the first requisite in a young man or woman for a successful career?"

Throughout the hundreds of replies ran a thread of thought most concisely expressed in the reply of a well-known sculptor: "Find out what work you like to do best, and do it all the time." *Sunshine Magazine*

# The Only Way to Get Together

□ "If you come at me with your fists doubled," Woodrow Wilson said, "I think I can promise you that mine will double as fast as yours, but if you come at me and say, 'Let us sit down and take counsel together, and, if we differ from one another, understand why it is that we differ from one another, just what the points at issue are,' we will presently find that we are not so far apart after all; that the points on which we differ are few and the points on which we agree are many; and that if we only have the patience and the candor and the desire to get together, we will get together."

\* \* \*

# Priceless Treasurers

□ The late George Horace Lorimer, for many years editor of the now defunct *Saturday Evening Post,* once wrote these words: "It is a good thing to have money, and the things that money can buy; but it is good, too, to check up once in a while and make sure we haven't lost the things that money can't buy."

The things that money cannot buy would make a long list. Here are some of them:

Money cannot buy real friendship; it must be earned.

Money cannot buy a clear conscience; square dealing is the price tag.

Money cannot buy the glow of good health; right living is the secret.

Money cannot buy happiness; happiness is a mental attitude, and one may be as happy in a cottage as in a mansion.

Money cannot buy sunsets, singing birds, and the music of the wind in the trees; these are as free as the air we breathe.

Money cannot buy inward peace; peace is the result of a constructive philosophy of life.

Money cannot buy character; character is what we are when we are alone with ourselves in the dark.

Continue the list yourself. You will agree that among the things money cannot buy are some of the most valuable treasures life has to offer. It is a good thing to check up now and then to be sure we are not missing these things. *Sunshine Magazine*

# Example

□ Example is not the main thing in influencing others. It is the only thing. *Albert Schweitzer*

# Relativity of Time

□ It took 5,000 years to progress from the sail to steam;
130 years from steam to gas, electricity, etc.;
40 years from gas, electricity, etc., to the atomic age;
12 years from the atomic age to the space age.
Note that the time span decreases as progress increases.

# On Living

□ I am unwilling to mix my fortune with him that is going down
the wind.                                              *Samuel Pepys*

# Deeds

◻ But the good deed, through the ages
Living in historic pages,
Brighter grows and gleams immortal,
Unconsumed by moth or rust.
                        *Henry Wadsworth Longfellow*

\* \* \*

◻ Whene'er a noble deed is wrought,
Whene'er is spoken a noble thought,
Our hearts, in glad surprise,
To higher levels rise.
                        *Henry Wadsworth Longfellow*

# One Person You Can't Fool

□ I have to live with myself, and so
I want to be fit for myself to know.
I want to be able, as days go by,
Always to look myself straight in the eye;
I don't want to stand, with the setting sun,
And hate myself for the things I've done.

I want to go out with my head erect,
I want to deserve all men's respect;
For here in the struggle for fame and self,
I want to be able to like myself.
I don't want to look at myself and know
That I'm bluster and bluff and empty show.
I never can hide myself from me;
I see what others may never see,
I know what others may never know.
I never can fool myself, and so,
Whatever happens I want to be
Self-respecting and conscience free.

*Anonymous*

# Long Live America

□ Next to God, the most sacred word in all the world to me is America. When I hear that word, something begins singing in my heart and sometimes the tears come in my eyes. I am not ashamed of those tears. For in that one word, America, are enshrined all my love, my dreams, my hopes, my faith in a future when not only I but all men shall be free. Who would not fight and if need be die for this blessed land of ours? Long live America.

*Unknown American Immigrant*

# Happiness

□ It is not how much we have, but how much we enjoy it, that makes for happiness.

# Acts the Best

□ We live in deeds, not years; in thoughts, not breaths;
In feelings, not in fingers on a dial.
We should count time by heart-throbs. He most lives
Who thinks most, feels the noblest, acts the best.

*P. J. Bailey*

# Successful Living

◻ Conrad N. Hilton, the well-known hotel executive, is credited with the following ten rules for successful living:

"Find your own particular talent. Be big. Be honest. Live with enthusiasm. Don't let your possessions possess you. Don't worry about your problems. Look up to people when you can—down to no one. Don't cling to the past. Assume your full share of responsibility in the world. Pray consistently and confidently."

# Contentment

◻ Happiness depends, as Nature shows,
  Less on exterior things than most suppose.        *William Cowper*

# Learn to Like These Things

◻ In these days of unrest and uncertainties, those who cultivate calmness and self-possession will live longer and enjoy life better. Hence, someone has collated a number of precepts to practice, as follows:

Learn to like what does not cost much.

Learn to like reading, conversation, music.

Learn to like plain food, plain service, plain cooking.

Learn to like people, even though some of them may be very different from you.

Learn to keep your wants simple. Refuse to be owned and anchored by things and opinions of others.

Learn to like the sunrise and the sunset, the beating of rain on the roof and windows, and the gentle fall of snow in winter.

Learn to like life for its own sake.        *Sunshine Magazine*

# Service

◻ I don't know what your destiny will be, but one think I know: the only ones among you who will be really happy are those who have sought and found how to serve.        *Albert Schweitzer*

# Happy Is the Man

□ Happy is the man who believes in God despite the seas of sadness that sometimes surround the lighthouse.

Happy is the man who believes in the greatness of America despite the poverty and prejudice that affect the fringes of our citizenry.

Happy is the man who believes in law and order despite crime in the streets and indifferences in the home.

Happy is the man who believes in the innate goodness of people, despite the vanity and greed of a small minority.

Happy is the man who believes in his own community, despite some blighted areas and the frustration of trying to clean them up.

Happy is the man who believes in himself, despite his known weaknesses and futile attempts to correct them.

Finally, happy is the man who believes, for in his belief lies his strength, his chances of success, and his realization of a rich, full life. *Sunshine Magazine*

# Just Thinking

□ Nobody can really guarantee the future. The best we can do is size up the chances, calculate the risks involved, estimate our ability to deal with them, and then make our plans with confidence. *Henry Ford II*

# Happiness

□ It has been proved over and over again that if you set out simply to find happiness, you never find it. Just as you think you have it in your grasp it eludes you. It is only when you abandon the idea and set out to make other people happy, to do good unselfishly, that you suddenly discover that you are really happy at last.

In helping others to happiness we are on the road to the same goal ourselves.

*The Late Richard Cardinal Cushing,*
*Archbishop of Boston*

# Trials

□ The diamond cannot be polished without friction, nor the man perfected without trials.                                    *Chinese Proverb*

* * *

□ Most of the grand truths of God have to be learned by trouble; they must be burned into us by the hot iron of affliction, otherwise we shall not truly receive them.     *Charles Haddon Spurgeon*

# Come Up Higher

□ I saw the mountains stand
Silent, wonderful and grand,
Looking out across the land
When the golden light was falling
On distant dome and spire,
And I heard a low voice calling,
"Come up higher. Come up higher;
From the lowlands and the mire,
From the mist of earth-desire,
From the vain pursuit of pelf,
From the attitude of self,
Come up higher. Come up higher."
                                            *James G. Clark*

# Honesty

□ Perfection is not necessarily a prerequisite to successful leadership. But honesty is.

# All Men as Friends

□ As we go out among men to do our work, touching the hands and lives of our fellows, make us, we pray thee, friends of all the world. Save us from blighting the fresh flower of any heart by the

257

flare of sudden anger or secret hate. May we not bruise the rightful self-respect of any by contempt or malice. Help us to cheer the suffering by our sympathy, to freshen the drooping by our hopefulness, and to strengthen in all the wholesome sense of worth and the joy of life. Save us from the deadly poison of class pride. Grant that we may look all men in the face with the eyes of a brother. If any needs us, make us ready to yield our help, ungrudgingly, unless higher duties claim us, and may we rejoice that we have it in us to be helpful to our fellowmen.

*Walter Rauschenbusch*

# Each Must Arise

□ The child, the seed, the grain of corn,
The acorn on the hill,
Each for some separate end is born
In season fit, and still
Each must in strength arise to work the
Almighty will.

*Robert Louis Stevenson*

# Learning to Live

□ As we learn to walk by walking, to leap by leaping, and to fence by fencing, so you can learn to live nobly only by acting nobly on every occasion that presents itself.     *J. S. Blackie*

# An Arabian Proverb

□ He who knows not, and knows not that he knows not; he is a fool, shun him.

He who knows not, and knows that he knows not; he is simple, teach him.

He who knows, and knows not that he knows; he is asleep, wake him.

He who knows, and knows that he knows; he is wise, follow him.

# Forward-Looking Hearts

□ O Thou great Master, who seest us in this school of life, rouse in us the heart to learn Thy lessons, to see the meaning of the story of mankind. Teach us the language of truth and courtesy. May experience bring us wisdom. May we be guided by the counsel of Thy love. Steady us through the discipline of disappointment. May mysteries not discourage but stir us. Make us patient to advance step by step. By the light of today may we undertake today's task, and may tomorrow find us ready for the next step. Deliver us from morbidness about yesterday and give us forward-looking hearts. Help us by obedience to keep open the new vision, and by action to make effective the new lesson. Let impulse blossom into resolve and bear fruit in deed. May the torch of truth pass from our hand to the hand of those who follow us, brightly burning, honorably kept, and at last may we hear Thy voice saying, "Well done, enter thou into the joy of thy Lord."

*Boyd Edwards, Prayer of the Hill School*

# They Will Climb

□ Where I lie down worn out, other men will stand young and fresh. By the steps that I have cut they will climb; by the stairs that I have built they will mount. They will never know the name of the man who made them. At the clumsy work they will laugh; when the stones roll they will curse me. But they will mount, and on my work; they will climb, and by my stair! . . . And no man liveth to himself, and no man dieth to himself!

*Olive Schreiner*

# A School Prayer

□ O God, Thou alone canst uphold the minds of men, without whose beauty and goodness our souls are unfed, without whose truthfulness our reasons wither, consecrate our lives to Thy will, giving us such purity of heart, such depth of faith, such steadfastness of purpose, that we may come to think Thy thoughts after Thee. *Groton School Prayers*

# For Graduates

□ O God, we pray Thee to send Thy blessing to all those who have gone forth from this school. Strengthen them in time of temptation. Be ever near them to comfort and support them and grant that in all they think or do or say they may live in Thy sight and service. *Frederick H. Sill, Kent School Prayers*

# Direction in Life

□ I find the great thing in this world is not so much where we stand as in what direction we are moving. *Oliver Wendell Holmes*

# Better than Gold

□ Happy is the man that findeth wisdom,
And the man that getteth understanding.
For the gaining of it is better than the gaining of silver,
And the profit thereof than fine gold.
She is more precious than rubies:
And none of the things thou canst desire are
  to be compared unto her.
Length of days is in her right hand:
In her left hand are riches and honor.
Her ways are ways of pleasantness,
And all her paths are peace.
She is a tree of life to them that lay hold upon her:
And happy is everyone that retaineth her.
Then shalt thou walk in thy way securely,
And thy foot shall not stumble. *Proverbs 3:13-18, 23*

# Be Helpful

□ Be silent when your words would hurt. Be patient when your neighbor's curt. Be deaf when gossip and scandal flow. Be thoughtful for another's woe. Be prompt when stern duty calls and be courageous when misfortune falls.

# Learning

□ A man learns only by two things: one is reading and the other is association with smarter people. *Will Rogers*

\* \* \*

□ We learn by trial and error. And if we have the capacity to learn by trial and error, then on the whole it is well with us.

\* \* \*

□ It is only those who refuse to learn that get into greater difficulties. *Nehru*

\* \* \*

□ What will a child learn sooner than a song? *Alexander Pope*

# To Serve

□ Teach us, good Lord, to serve Thee as Thou deservest; to give and not to count the cost; to fight and not to heed the wounds; to toil and not to seek for rest; to labor and not to ask for any reward, save that of knowing that we do Thy will.

*Ignatius Loyola*

# To a Son

□ My son, remember you have to work. Whether you handle pick or wheelbarrow or a set of books, dig ditches or edit a newspaper, ring an auction bell or write funny things, you must work.

Don't be afraid of killing yourself by overworking on the sunny side of thirty. Work gives you appetite for your meals; it lends solidity to your slumber; it gives you a perfect appreciation of a holiday.

There are young men who do not work, but the country is not proud of them. It does not even know their names, it only speaks of them as So-and-So's boys. Nobody likes them; the great, busy world doesn't know they are here.

So find out what you want to be and do. Take off your coat and make dust in the world. The busier you are, the less harm you are apt to get into, the sweeter will be your sleep, the brighter your holidays, and the better satisfied the whole world will be with you.                    *Bob Burdette in* Praying Hands

* * *

Imagination lit every lamp in this country, produced every article we use, built every church, made every discovery, performed every act of kindness and progress, created more and better things for more people. It is the priceless ingredient for a better day.                              *Henry J. Taylor*

# Think About These Things

☐ Finally, brethren, whatever is true, whatever is honorable, whatever is just, whatever is pure, whatever is lovely, whatever is gracious, if there is any excellence, if there is anything worthy of praise, think about these things.                    *Philippians 4:8*

# Graduation Prayer

☐ Our Father in Heaven; at this quiet hour (when the shadows are lengthening), help us to know what joy and peace come from seeking the secret places of the Most High. And as we pass out from this sheltered retreat of friendship and learning, grant that we may take with us high and helpful ideals that will aid us in combating the forces of evil that beset us. May we learn to look upon Thee as our shield and buckler, our strong defender.

*Charles L. Swift, Prayer of The Hill School*

# Prayer

☐ Prayers should be the key of the day and the lock of the night.

*English Proverb*

# Conservation

◻ Conservation teaches the principles of wise stewardship. It is truly ethical, because it counsels foresight in place of selfishness, vision in place of greed, and reverence in place of destructiveness.

*Canadian Wildlife*

# There Is a Life

◻ There is a life that is worth living now as it was worth living in the former days, and that is the honest life, the useful life, the unselfish life, cleansed by devotion to an ideal. There is a battle worth fighting now as it was worth fighting then, and that is the battle for justice and equality; to make our city and our state free in fact as well as in name; to break the rings that strangle real liberty, and to keep them broken; to cleanse, so far as in our power lies, the fountains of our national life from political, commercial, and social corruption; to teach our sons and daughters, by precept and example, the honor of serving such a country as America. That is work worthy of the finest manhood and womanhood.

*Henry Van Dyke*

# Revenge

◻ Revenge does us more harm than the injury of itself.

*John Lubbock*

# Patriotism

◻ Man has made remarkable strides in conquering outer space . . . but how futile have been his efforts in conquering inner space . . . the space in the heart and minds of men.

No people in all history—nor in any other land—has more avenues for individual expression . . . for influence . . . for persuasion than do the citizens of this nation.

The strongest influence is at the individual level. And the most effective influence is through personal example.

You have the power . . . use it.

263

We need more than military strength. We need moral strength. We need willpower. We need conviction and determination and dedication. These are individual strengths that cannot be generated by military leaders . . . nor by political leaders. This kind of power and strength must come from the brains and the hearts of the people. Must come from you and me.

This is both the test and the power of our system. Our national strength comes not from our political leaders . . . but from the hundred and ninety million citizens who have never failed our Constitutional principles in an hour of crisis.

To preserve this strength at the individual level, we must strive to improve our communications at the individual level. We must each reaffirm our faith in our way of life.

There are those who say we have no ideology to match the promise and the hope of the Communists.

I say, let them read again the Declaration of Independence. Let them carefully and thoughtfully study the story of our Constitution and our Bill of Rights. These are the instruments of our national strength . . . and of our individual strength. These are the flags that kindled hope in the hearts of oppressed peoples for a century and a half.

Let us again communicate these truths to our own people . . . and to our neighbors. *Charles L. Gould, Publisher,* San Francisco Examiner

# Home

□ A house is built by human hands, but a home is built by human hearts.

* * *

□ The strength of a nation is derived from the integrity of its homes. *Confucius*

# Help Where You Are

□ Because there is a good deal of the child in us, we grow impatient easily and say to ourselves, "Oh, if we could stand in the

264

lot of our more fortunate neighbors, we could live better, happier and more useful lives." Often we hear a young man say, "If I had the opportunity of my boss's son, I could achieve great success"; "If I didn't have to associate with such vulgar folk, I could become morally strong," says another; and a third laments, "If I only had the money of my wealthy friend, I should gladly do my part in the uplift of the world."

Now I am as much up in arms against needless poverty and degrading influences as anyone else, but, at the same time, I believe human experience teaches that if we cannot succeed in our present position, we could not succeed in any other. Unless, like the lily, we can rise pure and strong above sordid surroundings, we would probably be moral weaklings in any situation. Unless we can help the world where we are, we could not help it if we were somewhere else. *Helen Keller in* The Sea Breeze

# Sundial Motto

□ *Horas non numero nisi serenas* is the motto of a sundial near Venice. There is a softness and harmony in the words and in the thought unparalleled. Of all conceits it is surely the most classical. "I count only the hours that are serene."

*William Hazlitt (1778-1832)*

# Happiness

□ To enjoy happiness, we must create it. We should live simply, expect little, give much. We should fill our lives with love, scatter sunshine, forget self, and think of others. That is, do as we would be done by. Suppose we try it a week—see if we regret it.

*Praying Hands*

# A Modern Parable

□ Once there was a little boy. When he was three weeks old his parents turned him over to a baby-sitter.

When he was two years old, they dressed him up like a cowboy, and gave him a gun.

When he was three, everybody said, "Ain't he cute!" as he went about lisping a beer commercial.

When he was six, his father occasionally dropped him off at Sunday school on his way to the golf course across town.

When he was eight, they bought him a BB gun, and taught him to shoot sparrows. He learned to shoot windshields by himself.

When he was ten, he spent his afternoon time squatting at the drugstore newsstand reading comic books. His mother wasn't home, and his father was busy.

When he was thirteen, he told his parents other boys stayed out as late as they wanted to, so they said he could, too. It was easier that way.

When he was fifteen, the police called his home one night. "We have your boy. He's in trouble."

"In trouble?" screamed his father. "It can't be my boy!"

But it was.                                      *Sunshine Magazine*

# Beautiful Words

□ The ten most beautiful words in the English language—"beautiful in meaning and in the musical arrangement of their letters"—as compiled by Wilfred J. Funk, poet and lexicographer, are: dawn, hush, lullaby, murmuring, tranquil, mist, luminous, chimes, golden, melody.

# Greatest Figure of the Age

□ Bernard Baruch once was asked who he thought was the greatest figure of the age. To this he replied:

"The fellow that does his job every day ... The mother who has children and gets up and gets breakfast and keeps them clean and sends them off to school ... The fellow who keeps the streets clean—without him we wouldn't have any sanitation ... The Unknown Soldier ... Millions of men."

Those who carry out unexciting, but essential, jobs are often among the most important contributors to humanity in the long run.

One reason such persons seldom receive recognition—or even

266

thanks—is that there are so many of them. Their ordinariness does not detract from the fact that, without their prompt, thorough and devoted performance, everybody suffers.

You have been commissioned by God to carry out an assignment in life that He has given to no one else. How well you do it counts for time and eternity.

*"Three Minutes a Day,"*
*Reverend James Keller in* Praying Hands.

# Two Can Handle It

◻ An old preacher greeted each new day with: "O Lord, help me to remember that nothing is going to happen to me today that You and I together can't handle."  *Praying Hands*

# Youth's Credo

◻ I believe in the greatness of myself, and that I am in this world for a purpose, that purpose being to put back into life more than I have taken out.

I believe in the integrity of other people, assured that they try as hard to follow the gleam, even as I.

I believe in the gallantry of older people whose seasoned experience and steadfast devotion have preserved for me the precious heritage of the past.

I believe in the magnificence of the past, knowing that without its storied wealth I would possess nothing.

I believe in the challenge of the future, fully realizing there will be no future except it becomes alive through me.

I believe in the sacredness of duty, through which I must do those things that are expected of me, and above all, fulfill the purpose for which I am here.

I believe in the nobility of work as the creative expression of the best within me, and as my share in easing the common load of all.

I believe in the enrichment of play and laughter as the means of cleansing my body of staleness and my mind of dullness.

I believe in the contagion of health, and that I can spread it through cheerfulness, wholesome habits, sensible expenditure of energies, and wise use of foods.

I believe in the holiness of friendship, knowing that my life is a tapestry woven from the threads of many beautiful lives.

Because I believe these things, I therefore believe in God, who justifies all my beliefs: He is the still small voice within, ever urging me toward the unattained. Since He cares for these things, I believe that even death cannot steal these priceless possessions from me.

And whatever more I believe is entwined in those precious feelings that lie too deep for words!

*W. Waldemar W. Argow in* Sunshine Magazine

## A Great Change

☐ I was brought up in a family where there was never any talk about God. But when I became a grown-up person I found that it was impossible to exist without God in one's heart. I came to that conclusion myself, without anybody's help or preaching. But that was a great change because since that moment the main dogmas of Communism lost their significance for me.

*Svetlana Alliluyeva, daughter of Stalin*

## Rights

☐ Every man has a right to his opinion, but no man has a right to be wrong in his facts. *Bernard Baruch*

## A Prayer for Americans

☐ Give us an understanding heart. Then shall we realize the needs and the aspirations of our brother mortals. Give us the will and the zeal and the strength to encourage and succor. Save us from indifference and indolence.

Give us faith in the worthiness of our purpose so we may never doubt that the seeds we sow shall blossom into fruit.

Let nothing daunt or discourage us.

May our aim be less to win gratitude than to further the good and the happiness of our fellow beings. Teach us to forget unworthy self-interest, but to give unselfish service, so we may truly learn that he who would lose his life shall save it and that he who would save his life shall lose it.

Open our eyes to the unnumbered opportunities lying at hand for unspectacular daily service, and give us the secret satisfaction that comes from not letting the right hand know what the left hand is doing for others.

Reveal to us the emptiness and the hollowness of public applause that does not ring true in our inner consciousness.

Preserve us from all cowardice, save the cowardice that would check us from attempting to promote our own interest at the expense of another's.

Prosper our undertakings if they make for the welfare of the world, but thwart them if their influence upon mankind be hurtful; that we may thereby be induced to take our bearings afresh and alter our course. *B. C. Forbes*

# True Nobility

□ There is nothing noble in being superior to some other man. True nobility is being superior to your previous self. *Seneca*

# Flag Day

□ Of the thousands of words written about the Flag of the United States of America, some have stood through the passing years:

Charles Sumner, in 1867: "There is the Flag. He must be cold, indeed, who can look upon its folds rippling in the breeze without feeling pride of country."

Woodrow Wilson, in 1912: "I cannot look upon the Flag without imagining that it consists of alternate stripes of parchment upon which are written the fundamental rights of man, alternating with the streams of blood by which those rights have been vindicated and validated. . . . The things that the Flag stands for were created by the experiences of a great people. Everything that it stands for was written by their lives. The Flag is the embodiment, not of sentiment, but of history."

Theodore Roosevelt in 1917: "We can have no 'fifty-fifty' allegiance in this country. Either a man is an American and nothing else, or he is not an American at all. We are akin by blood and descent to most of the nations of Europe; but we are separate from all of them . . . and we are bound always to give our whole-hearted and undivided loyalty to our own Flag."

Over the years, the Flag has continued to have profound meaning for most Americans. When we celebrate Flag Day on June 14, let us pay homage to the "Flag of Freedom," with fitting and reverent tributes.

Let's fly it proudly! *Sunshine Magazine*

# Talent

◻ I think this is the most extraordinary collection of talent, of human knowledge, that has ever been gathered together at the White House—with the possible exception of when Thomas Jefferson dined alone.

*Statement by John F. Kennedy*
*at a dinner in the White House*
*for American Nobel Prize winners,*
*April 29, 1962*

# The Universe—Creation or Chance?

◻ The former president of the New York Academy of Science, Dr. A. Cressy Morrison, declares that it is possible to demonstrate mathematically that the universe could not have just happened or evolved. He says it shows such definite design and purpose that it demands a "Master Mind" to account for its many perfections.

He points out that the earth rotates on its axis at 1,000 miles an hour. If it rotated at only 100 miles an hour, our days and nights would be ten times as long as they are now, and the earth would alternately burn and freeze. Under such circumstances vegetation could not live.

He notes, too, that the sun has a surface temperature of 12,000 degrees Fahrenheit and that our earth is at the exact distance necessary to get just enough heat, and yet not too much.

Our globe is tilted at an angle of 23 degrees, and this enables us to have four seasons; if it were not tilted at this angle, vapors from the ocean would move north and south, piling up continents of ice.

If the moon were not the exact distance that it is from the earth, the ocean tides would inundate the land completely twice a day.

If the ocean were a few feet deeper than it is, the carbon dioxide and the oxygen in the earth's atmosphere would be completely absorbed and no vegetable life could exist on the earth.

If the atmosphere were just a little thinner, many of the meteors, which are now harmlessly burned up in space, would bombard us, setting great fires everywhere.

Did this delicate balance just happen? Not a chance in ten million!

As we delve into the intricate and marvelous designs of the Universe, we exclaim with the psalmist: "O Lord, how manifold are thy works! in wisdom hast thou made them all." (Psalm 104:24). *These Times*

# Despondence

□ Because you have occasional low spells of despondence, don't despair. The sun has a sinking spell every night, but it rises again all right the next morning. *Henry Van Dyke*

# Youth and Old Age

□ Youth is not entirely a time of life; it is a state of mind. It is not wholly a matter of ripe cheeks. It is a temper of the will, a quality of the imagination, a vigor of the emotions, a freshness of the deep springs of life. It means a temperamental predominance of courage over timidity, of an appetite for adventure over love of ease. Nobody grows old by merely living a number of years.

People grow old only by deserting their ideals. Years may wrinkle the skin, but to give up interest wrinkles the soul. Worry, doubt, self-distrust, fear, and despair—these are the long, long years that bow the head and turn the growing spirit back to dust.

Whatever your years, there is in every being's heart the love of wonder, the undaunted challenge of events, the unfailing childlike appetite for what next, and the joy in the game of life. You are as young as your faith, as old as your fear, as young as your hope, as old as your despair.

In the central place of every heart there is a recording chamber; so long as it receives messages of beauty, hope, cheer and courage—so long are you young. When the wires are all down and your heart is covered with the snows of pessimism and the ice of cynicism—then, and then only, are you grown old.

*General Douglas MacArthur*
*on his seventy-fifth birthday*

## Values

□ What we obtain too cheap, we esteem too lightly; it is dearness only that gives everything its value.          *Thomas Paine*

## Wisdom—Our Greatest Asset

□ It isn't quite true that youth is our country's greatest asset. Wisdom is our greatest asset, and wisdom is gained through experience in schools. Our youth must get their training and experience—preparation in high schools and colleges today.

*Walter H. Judd, physician and former Congressman*

## Foundation

□ The bricklayer laid a brick on the bed of cement. Then, with a precise stroke of his trowel spread another layer, and without a by-your-leave, laid on another brick. The foundations grew visibly . . . the building rose, tall and strong, to shelter men.

I thought, Lord, of that brick, buried in the darkness at the base

272

of the big building. No one sees it, but it accomplishes its task, and the other bricks need it. Lord, what does it matter whether I am on the rooftop or in the foundations of your building, so long as I stand faithfully at the place where You want me to be?

*The Anglican Digest*

# The Best Things

□ The best things are the nearest:
breath in your nostrils,
light in your eyes,
flowers at your feet,
duties at your hand,
the path of Right just before you.
Do not grasp at the stars,
but do life's plain, common work
as it comes,
certain that daily duties and daily bread
are the sweetest things of life.

*Robert Louis Stevenson*

# The Complexity of Society

□ I've long thought that the humorists of each generation have managed to capture best what is about to worry us all. Certainly the two best humorists of my youth, E. B. White and James Thurber, both somehow captured and expressed the worry about complexity that is now bugging us all, and is somehow not quite so comic as it used to be. In a 1927 story in the *New Yorker*, E. B. White had one of his characters say, "I predict a bright future for complexity in the United States of America." Then he went on to ask a question which I commend to you for those moments in the middle of the night when you wake up and are trying to think what it is you ought to think of: "Have you ever considered how complicated things could get, what with one thing leading to another?"

Thurber wasn't afraid of complexity as White was. He just loved it; he was more like a little boy rushing into a dirty puddle. But both humorists were obsessed with it, and now it obsesses us all. And so the complications that we are now heir to evoke in us a kind of sardonic smile about something that we once heard and laughed at. The complex of relationships which have come to be called the generation gap evoke that classic line from a Damon Runyon story. " 'Shut up,' my father explained." The frustrations of complexity on the highways remind us of that memorable lady who, arrested on a one-way street going the wrong way, said to the policeman, "Officer, have you considered that that arrow may be pointing the wrong way?" She was speaking, wasn't she, for all of us and not only about traffic.

*Excerpts from an address*
*at Northern Illinois University*
*by Harlan Cleveland,*
*President of the University of Hawaii*

## Alluring Temptations

□ Many a dangerous temptation comes to us in fine gay colours that are but skin-deep. *Matthew Henry*

## A Voice from On High

□ From a diary of a young soldier killed in action in World War II as printed in *Life Magazine:* "This is a time for a new revelation. People don't think much about religion nowadays, but we need a voice from on high, brother, and I don't mean maybe! This thing has got out of human ability to run. I'm no religious fanatic, but we're in a situation where something better than human brains has got to give us advice."

## Most of the News That's Fit to Print Never Gets Printed

□ More than 250,000 college students in this country operate, without pay, 1000 programs for mentally retarded children, others conduct classes in hospitals and jails, still others tutor ghetto children to enable them to keep up with children from more fortunate homes.

More than 200 American corporations donate tools and money to 140 schools in Latin America training 150,000 students to earn a self-supporting, self-respecting future more friendly to the United States.

In 160 American cities 18,800 businessmen act as Big Brothers to young boys who lack and desperately need that sort of counsel, friendliness, help.

In Michigan a small group of students donated and collected money to pay merchants for windows broken by student rioters.

Marines in Vietnam, out of their own pockets, have built and maintain three hospitals for natives; regularly provide toys for hundreds of children who never had any; encouraged and helped an American town, from which one Marine had come, to give a Christmas to the entire Vietnam town in defense of which he had been killed.

Large corporations have set up and maintain in Harlem a very special school for drop-outs, to fit them for college. There have been no drop-outs from that school.

So be of good cheer . . . it's still America—and it's wonderful.

*An advertisement*
*of the Warner and Swazey Company,*
*Cleveland, Ohio*

# Faith

□ Faith in a supreme being is probably the most difficult thing for many people to accept, and if there is any way I can help someone to discover faith, then that's the most important thing I could ever do.　　　*Randy Hundley, catcher for the Chicago Cubs*

# Words of Wisdom

□ While still a young man, I was at my work bench one day filing a piece of metal. I was working hard with vigorous but very short strokes. My boss came along, saw what I was doing and said, "Both ends of that file are paid for. Don't take those short strokes with the middle of the file, use both ends." I wonder if we don't often make that mistake in life. It is commonly acknowledged that we probably don't use more than a small percentage of the potential with which God has endowed us. By His grace, let's take broader strokes, be more effective by utilizing *all* of our time, talent, and treasures for the Lord. Let's use both ends of the file.

*R. G. LeTourneau*

# Most Richly Blessed!

☐ I asked God for strength, that I might achieve
—I was made weak, that I might learn
humbly to obey. . .
I asked for health, that I might do greater
things—I was given infirmity, that I might do
better things . . .
I asked for riches, that I might be happy—I
was given poverty, that I might be wise . . .
I asked for power, that I might have the praise
of men—I was given weakness, that I might feel
the need of God . . .
I asked for all things, that I might enjoy life—
I was given life, that I might enjoy all things . . .
I got nothing that I asked for—but everything
I had hoped for . . .
Almost despite myself, my unspoken prayers
were answered. I am, among all men, most
richly blessed! *Prayer written by a Confederate soldier*

# The Happiest Persons

☐ Some years ago a London newspaper offered prizes for the best answers to this question: "Who are the happiest persons on earth?" The answers were so surprising and encouraging that we like to reprint them occasionally. Here are the four answers which were adjudged the best:
  "A craftsman or artist whistling over a job well done."
  "A little child building sand castles."

"A mother, after a busy day, bathing her baby."

"A doctor who has finished a difficult and dangerous operation, and saved a human life."

What? No playboys? No millionaires? No international jet-setters? No kings? No Hollywood idols? No addicts high on drugs? Looks as if kicks, riches, fame, and rank are not rated so highly as essentials of a happy life. Plainly the decision is that happiness is for everybody, not for just a priviledged few. If no one but the glamorous and the rich could be happy, then the rest of us might have real grounds for complaint.

But that doesn't seem to be the case, does it? *Nuggets*

# Honor

□ No person was ever honored for what he received. Honor has been the reward for what he gave. *Calvin Coolidge*

# Faith

□ "It takes no brains to be an atheist. Any stupid person can deny the existence of a supernatural power because man's physical senses cannot detect it. But there cannot be ignored the influence of conscience, the respect we feel for moral law, the mystery of first life on what once must have been a molten mass, or the marvelous order in which the universe moves about us on this earth. All of these evidence the handiwork of a beneficent Deity. For my part, that Deity is the God of the Bible and of Christ, His Son." *Dwight D. Eisenhower*

# Standing on Your Own Feet

□ Everyone who leaves school or university this year is looking forward to standing on his own feet and making his own way in the world.

Benjamin Franklin was of the opinion that a ploughman on his feet is higher than a gentleman on his knees, and one of the

277

characters in Ibsen's play, *An Enemy of the People* says: "The strongest man in the world is he who stands most alone."

But before you can stand on your own feet you must have something more in your head than the desire to stand up. You need to know enough to keep your balance. That is why young people go to school and university and church; that is why wise older people keep learning by reading and observing. In this changing world it is not enough to have in your head nothing more than was there yesterday.

No person can be completely sovereign in the sense that he is in no way affected by what happens outside himself. Independence must walk hand in hand with knowledge of what is going on, intelligent obedience to certain laws of life, and fidelity to certain customs of humanity.

The advice given a thousand years ago, "Be yourself," has been translated in these days into "Do your own thing." Some people draw attention to themselves by a lavish display of qualities, like a storekeeper who thinks he has to crowd into his window everything he has to sell, or like a flower arranger trying to cram all of her garden into a table vase.

What is the basic imperative of life, the compulsion that makes one want to stand up? It is a paltry ambition if one's sole purpose in standing up is to display a suit or a dress.

A book on social pathology lists as the prime wishes of most individuals: new experiences, security, response and recognition. How insular and selfish these appear when they are compared with the ambition to contribute something constructive to the human experience. No person enjoys the greatest happiness possible to him unless he is able to say: "I am paying my way in the human scene." This is a satisfaction that cannot be matched by any social status or any standard of living, however high.

Anyone who is worried about his lack of advancement in social or business life might well take a few minutes to think up the answer to: "What motivates me?" Motivation may consist of the urge to succeed, to climb to the top of a mountain and add your stone to the cairn there, or it may be a longing to add something to the beauty of life through one of the arts.

Most important is what follows: to work intelligently toward the objective under one's own power. One simple objective for everyone is to become all that he can become, to progress from what is passable to what is excellent, and from what youth yearned for to what maturity fulfills. The achievement applauded by the public or paid for by a corporation is dust and ashes in your mouth if you know that you could have done better. Thomas Fuller said this in a book he published in 1640: "Good is not good when proceeding from them from whom far better is expected."

*Royal Bank of Canada Monthly Letter*

## When Things Go Wrong

☐ When things go wrong as they sometimes will,
  When the road you're trudging seems all up hill,
  When the funds are low and the debts are high,
  And you want to smile, but you have to sigh,
  When care is pressing you down a bit,
  Rest if you must, but don't you quit.
  Life is queer with its twists and turns,
  As everyone of us sometimes learns,
  And many a failure turns about
  When he might have won had he stuck it out?
  Don't give up though the pace seems slow—
  You may succeed with another blow.
  Success is failure turned inside out—
  The silver tint of the clouds of doubt,
  And you never can tell how close you are,
  It may be near when it seems so far;
  So stick to the fight when you're hardest hit—
  It's when things seem worst that you must not quit.

*Author Unknown*

## Bottled Cucumbers

☐ "When I was a little boy," remarked an old man, "somebody gave me a cucumber in a bottle. The neck of the bottle was small, and the cucumber so large it wasn't possible for it to pass through, and I wondered how it got there. But out in the garden one day I came upon a bottle slipped over a little green fellow, and then I understood. The cucumber had grown in the bottle.

279

"Now I often see men with habits that I wonder any strong, sensible man could form, and then I think that likely they grew into them when they were young, and cannot slip out of them now. They are like the cucumber."

# Thanksgiving

□ Humbly before God and proudly before man,
we are grateful.
Thanksgiving is a time for remembering,
and what memories are ours!
We who dwell in a land where freedom
prevails and where honor and
righteousness is our code, remember
the solid foundation upon which
our nation is built.
As a people we stand united in an
effort to preserve that which
is our heritage.
For the opportunities and privileges
which have benefited us
as individuals and as a nation,
and for the blessings which
have been bestowed upon us,
we are grateful.
In our hearts we give thanks
that we can say to
all the world,
"I am an American!"

*Sunshine Magazine*

# Why Men Push On

□ Throughout the great farming sections of our country a few years ago, thousands of men worked hard and long, cultivating and sowing their lands only to have a devastating summer drought intercept their harvest and make worthless all of their wearing toil. Yet those men, undefeated by nature's cruel prank, and urged on by everlasting hope, when planting time returned, again flung seed into nature's bosom and pressed hoe and harrow into the soil of their lands. They represented an unconscious symbol of faith.

During depression years, millions of unemployed people kept the light of hope in their eyes, despite hardship and want. Hope alone made them look beyond unrest and insecurity, beyond the questionings and heartaches, the defeats and disappointments.

Hope is the greatest sustaining force in life. It is the one element in the human spirit that will not remain subdued by difficulties. Always it beckons toward the promised land. Man lives, struggles, suffers; he finds himself rebuffed, disillusioned, discouraged, and his efforts and labors wasted, only to have an inner voice tell him to go on, to take one more step, then another, and another.

The businessman, beset on all sides by worries and problems, the clerk behind the store counter, the doctor, the lawyer, the servant—all alike are pushed ahead in life by Hope. It was a wise Providence that planted Hope in the human breast. When everything else is gone Hope lingers on. Fortunately for man, it is the last thing to leave him—unless he himself casts it aside.

*Sunshine Magazine*

## Prayer

□ Every man prays in his own language, and I believe there is no language that God does not understand. Every time His children have thrown away fear in the pursuit of His word, miracles have happened. *Duke Ellington, musician, composer*

## 1,440

□ A man had a strange dream of an angel giving him this message: "As a reward for your virtues the sum of $1,440 will be deposited in the bank every morning for you. However, a condition is to be met. At the close of business each day, any balance not used is canceled. It cannot be carried over to the next day, but a new $1,440 will be credited to you."

This dream was so vivid that the man asked for a revelation of its meaning, and the answer came: Each morning life credited his account with 1,440 minutes; each night it canceled those not invested in some good purpose.

Each of us has such an account. At the close of "business" each day, can we look over our ledger for the day and honestly evaluate what we have done with our 1,440 golden minutes?

*Daily Word, Unity*

## Four Questions

□ An old fable has it that when God was creating the world He was approached by four questioning angels.

"How are you doing it?" the first one asked.

The second queried, "Why?"

The third one said, "May I have it when You finish?"

The fourth one said, "Can I help?"

The first one was the question of a scientist; the second, the philosopher's; the third, the selfish person's; and the fourth was the question of the religious one.        *Sunshine Magazine*

## Worn Testament Shows Student's Way

□ The crash of a chartered airplane in the Colorado Rockies took the lives of 31 football players, coaches and fans from Wichita State University, Wichita, Kansas. Among them was 19-year-old John Duren of Oklahoma City, Oklahoma, who in the words of his campus pastor "knew Christ as his constant friend, and now he walks with Christ in victory over death."

John left behind at the University United Methodist Church in Wichita a worn copy of "Good News for Modern Man," the Today's English Version New Testament published by the American Bible Society. The paperback was found with the lid of a paper cup inserted at pages 216-17, where he had underlined John 3:16: "For God loved the world so much that he gave his only Son, so that everyone who believes in him may not die but have eternal life."

John's copy of "Good News" was used to read "The Message in Scripture" at the Sunday services last December 6 at University United Methodist. Five Wichita State University football players participated in the services, including John's roommate last year who told that the two read from the TEV New Testament each evening. Said Pastor Richard E. Taylor, Jr.: "Johnny truly represented the best in youth, not a saint, but a seeking, asking, knocking university student."

American Bible Society Record

# Class Motto

□ A certain high school graduating class chose for its motto this profound truth:

Your Life is God's gift to you;
What you do with it is your gift to God. *Praying Hands*

# The Clock of Life

□ The clock of life is wound but once
And no man has the power
To tell just *when* the hands will stop—
At late or early hour.
*Now* is the only time you own;
Live, love, toil with a will—
Place no faith in "tomorrow" for
The clock may then be still.

*F.E.P. in* Praying Hands

# An Uncommon Man

□ It has been dinned into us that this is the Century of the Common Man.... Thus we are in danger of developing a cult ... of mediocrity. But ... most Americans ... will get mad and fight if you try calling them common.

This is hopeful because it shows that most people are holding fast to an essential fact in American life. We believe in equal opportunity for all, but we know that this includes the opportunity to rise to leadership—in other words, to be uncommon.

Let us remember that the great human advances have not been

brought about by mediocre men and women. They were brought about by distinctly uncommon people with vital sparks of leadership. . . .

It is a curious fact that when you get sick you want an uncommon doctor; if your car breaks down you want an uncommonly good mechanic; when we get into war we want dreadfully an uncommon admiral and an uncommon general. . . .

The future of America rests not in mediocrity, but in the constant renewal of leadership in every phase of our national life.

*Herbert Hoover,* This Week

## Some Difficult Things To Do

□ To admit guilt.
To break a habit.
To love an enemy.
To think logically.
To confess ignorance.
To withhold judgment.
To grow old gracefully.
To persevere without haste.
To wait without impatience.
To decide without prejudice.
To suffer without complaint.
To know when to keep silent.
To be indifferent to ridicule.
To hate the sin, yet love the sinner.
To concentrate in the midst of strife.
To endure hatred without resentment.
To fraternize without losing individuality.
To serve without compensation, commendation, recognition.

*Sunshine Magazine*

## More Time

□ Every person has a backlog of things he is going to do when he has "more time." Those two words are the most deceptive cheats in life. They seem to assure us that someday we will have more time. And nothing is further from the truth. The wise thing is to find "more time" by selective use of the hours and minutes of today to enjoy the things that appeal to you now.

# Importance

□ If we are to believe that there is any kind of order in the universe, we must also believe that every human life is important. Albert Schweitzer went even further when he spoke of a "reverence for all of life." This means that you are important. Your life is important. What you do is important to yourself and others. There may be those who feel that your accomplishments are humble or limited, but your very zest for life depends on maintaining the realization that your life has great meaning and importance. *The Word*

# I Am an American

□ I have died in Vietnam. But I have walked on the face of the moon.

I have befouled the waters and tainted the air of a magnificent land. But I have made it safe from disease.

I have flown through the sky faster than the sun. But I have idled in streets made ugly with traffic.

I have littered the land with garbage. But I have built upon it a hundred million homes.

I have divided schools with my prejudice. But I have sent armies to unite them.

I have beat down my enemies with clubs. But I have built courtrooms to keep them free.

I have built a bomb to destroy the world. But I have used it to light a light.

I have outraged my brothers in the alleys of the ghettos. But I have transplanted a human heart.

I have scribbled out filth and pornography. But I have elevated the philosophy of man.

I have watched children starve from my golden towers. But I have fed half of the earth.

I was raised in a grotesque slum. But I am surfeited by the silver spoon of opulence.

I live in the greatest country in the world in the greatest time in history. But I scorn the ground I stand upon.

I am ashamed.

But I am proud.

I am an American. *The Hearing Digest*

# The Poet's Prayer

□ If there be some weaker one,
   Give me strength to help him on;
   If a blinder soul there be,
   Let me guide him nearer Thee;
   Make my mortal dreams come true
   With the work I fain would do;
   Clothe with life the weak intent,
   Let me be the thing I meant;
   Let me find in Thy employ,
   Peace that dearer is than joy;
   Out of self to love be led,
   And to heaven acclimated,
   Until all things sweet and good
   Seem my natural habitude.
   *John Greenleaf Whittier*

DATE DUE